AGE OF MYSTERY

Sons of God, Daughters of Man,

And Tsz-Nephilimus Sapien

Dr. Harry Assad Salem III

AGE OF MYSTERY Sons of God, Daughters of Man, and Tsz-Nephiliums Sapien
ISBN 1-890370-36-3

Salem Family Ministries
PO Box 1595
Cathedral City, CA 92345
www.salemfamilyministries.org

Disclaimer: The views expressed in this book contain my personal opinions, theories, and experiences throughout my life and time spent in God's word and private research. I express them as my opinion and views only, and share them with you from my lifelong experience and research. I am only communicating what has been revealed to me, and what I have personally studied and researched.

DEDICATION

This book is dedicated to my niece Mia Gabrielle Salem, who kept me looking towards the future in order to look into the past.

CONTENTS

ACKNOWLEDGMENTS

I give acknowledgement to my Mi Mi, Patricia Salem White, who gave me the Salem Family Bible that greatly aided my research.

FORWARD

The world is a much bigger place than people often realize. One way to understand our larger world is to look at the things that most people often never pay attention to or see. The Bible is an example of ancient writings that contain mysteries that even the greatest of minds has yet to fully understand. If we looked at them like a little child, then we could begin to unlock the mysteries it contains.

Once we unlock those mysteries, then we can focus on matters elsewhere. The ancient world is full of wonders that humanity has only begun to even comprehend. They go back to the very foundations of the creation of the world. Humans once shared the world with multiple unique species including giants. Mankind interbred with the sons of God and produced offspring. Mankind had extinction level events just like the dinosaurs. These are just some of the wonders that will be revealed in the following pages.

Throughout each chapter is a detailed look into art, history, science, culture, civilization, military, mythology, and Biblical knowledge that has never been considered or discovered. Each discovery is a piece of a puzzle that fits together all the missing parts of life that has often been cast aside as irrelevant or not important to look into for deeper study. To possess the right thinking for better understanding requires us to look at all the things that connect the dots of the unknown. If we were to look at the word 'apocalypse' in the original Greek meaning of the word for example, then we would see that the word is defined as to reveal. Many people make the mistake of associating the word apocalypse with destruction the end of the world. Revealing the definition of that one word apocalypse shows the point of just how important it is to see all the details of whatever subject someone is studying.

As we dwell into a deeper knowledge of God's great creation, then we will begin to unravel mysteries that perhaps would never come across our minds. It is vital to learn as much as humanly possible about everything. When understanding is attained, then wisdom and knowledge can be unlocked. This brings us into a spirit of excellence for bigger and greater things. The age of enlightenment begins with the age of beginnings.

CHAPTER 1: THEORIES AND IDEAS

When I look at the world, I see many different ideas of where humanity originated. Studying anthropology, archaeology, and theology gave me a fascination with learning truth and fact. With learning about my past as a human being, seeing all the underlying facts was vital to me knowing how to make the things I learned about absolute.

For most of my life, discovery was an essential part of my existence. While the rest of the world saw things one way, I looked at them from multiple directions. My time working in ministry and traveling the world was a way for me to grow more free and independent from the usual constraints of society. I was on the road with my family from a young age up until my late teens. This gave me the opportunity to see sites that few got to see, enjoy discoveries that were not always available in certain areas, and explore intrigues of mine almost anytime I wanted. I had the luxuries of a loving family, a good education, and a chance to grow in God. My deepness in God came in the form of my walk with Him, and knowledge that grew from studying Him and His word.

My experience in science stems from my education in anthropology and archaeology. Anthropology means the study of humanity. Archaeology means the study of human activity in the past, primarily through the recovery and analysis of the material, culture, and environmental data that has been left behind from ancient civilizations that include artifacts, architecture, and artwork. My areas of study focused on cultural anthropology, in which I received my degree, and biological anthropology where I learned to read what I call the human universe. This would be better known as biology, both ancient and modern. My archaeology expertise is not so much fixed in one field, but in multiple areas of study. This multi-field approach allowed me to learn at a fast rate while keeping a careful eye on details, facts, and clues of great and small size to further my work. My studies in geology, natural resources, history, and linguistics have also provided me with the skills and knowledge necessary to be an effective teacher of the mysteries of creation.

I learned to respect knowledge because it is unlimited. I realized that God always wanted His creation to have His knowledge and wisdom. It also brought great levels of responsibility and accountability. Mankind was never made to be perfect. We were made to be exactly like it says in Genesis 1:31, *"And God saw everything He had made, and behold it was very good (KJV)."* The mankind that God made was meant never to be perfect, but very good.

Mankind is not a flawed creation, yet it is not a perfect creation by any means. This is how we are perfect in God's eyes. We have the freedom to choose and rule our own destiny. This is a reason that we adapt, change, and evolve to a state of perfection, yet are never truly or ever will be truly perfect. To be absolutely perfect would dismiss the need for God as a loving creator, teacher, and father. It is this trait that God Himself, while still the only perfect being in existence, grows and changes as He continues to teach each and every single individual of His human creation. God's free will to teach and offer to help His precious creation grow and evolve to become more like Him is one of the ways we see His perfect nature. Free will is also how other human species came into existence.

The existence of humanity has spawned many different theories and beliefs about humanities origin. Two main beliefs on the beginnings of mankind exist in today's world. These are evolution and creationism. By definition, evolution is change in hereditary traits of biological populations over successive generations. The process of evolution gives rise in diversity at every available level of biological organization that includes species, organisms, and molecules on different levels, and individuality. Creationism is the belief that the universe and life originate from a divine creator or creation based on specific events.

This includes Biblical literacy beliefs as well as an inclusion of other religious and mythological ideologies. Predominately both fields of evolution and creationism are at constant odds with each other. Only on very rare occasions do they come together for such areas like theistic evolution, which is the view that God and modern science are compatible with biological evolution. This is a rejection of the conflict thesis that hold religion and science separate and instead embraces both in non-contradictory ways.

My personal opinion is that God developed mankind to adapt and grow with change. He made all life this way. One scripture I favor with this idea in mind is Romans 1:20 *"For the invisible things of Him from the creation of the world are clearly seen, being understood by they things that are made, even His eternal power and Godhead; so that they are without excuse* (KJV)*."* I see God's hand in everything that walks and talks on the face of the earth. I see God's creations adapt and grow to be better just like He had planned from the very beginning.

God designed all His creations to adapt to change. I see evidence of this throughout the Bible. In science books and magazines I read about life adapting to meet the changing times and environments. I use environments with an *s* for plural because each part of the world produces several different environmental conditions unique to the different areas of the earth. Weather patterns, climate changes, temperatures, and all other areas of nature are different throughout the world. This makes all things living adapt and change to current and future environmental differences in order to survive and thrive.

If we take into account the fact that the earth is dated to be millions to billions of years old, then it would only be natural to assume all life was designed to grow with changes, or to die out (become extinct) like dinosaurs and other species. The Bible itself, I have come to notice seems to possibly cover a timeline of over 10,000 years rather than the estimated 4,000 to 6,000 years time span many believe it covers historically.

Moses, the author of the first five books of the Bible called the Torah (six books possibly as he is believed to be the author of the book of Job) lived in a time when many histories and sciences were in existence throughout the early empires. Moses had access to them by way of his royal lineage as a member of the Egyptian royal family. It is plausible to say he was educated on civilizations, timelines, and the sciences of the day that only the most enlightened minds (scholars and tutors) would share with him due to his status as a prince of Egypt. Aside from Moses are other accounts spread throughout the Bible by the various authors. While more study needs to be done, I have come to the conclusion that the Bible spans a chronological events timeline of 10,000 years.

It is true that all life grows and changes over time. With each new generation of people born, differences are inherited via family traits and natural environment adapted attributes. Before and after the flood of Noah came a very different face upon the earth. The entirety of the book of Genesis describes the beginnings of life itself. The Genesis chapters of one and six give, in detail, the origins of early life through creation followed by an adaption to what mankind and the rest of the world would become today.

This idea of mankind evolving with each new generation plays out with evidence found in the book of Genesis. We see in chapter six of Genesis, using the English Standard Bible here and later the King James Bible, that there were two kinds of human species present. Genesis 6:4 in the English Standard Version give the account *"The Nephilim were on the earth in those days, and also afterward, when the sons of God came in to the daughters of man and bore children to them. These were the mighty men who were of old, the men of renown (ESV)."* The King James Version states, *"There were giants in the earth in those days; and also after that, when the sons of God came in unto the daughters of men, and they bare children to them, the same became mighty men which were of old, men of renown* (KJV)."

The presence of these men in the Bible gives evidence that there were other species of mankind on the earth. This does not mean that they were spawned outside of God's great creation by some random phenomenon, but rather by a joining or union of the bloodlines of God's created mankind and one other creation that God had made before humans. This other creation would be the sons of God, or in Hebrew the *Bene Elohim*. These sons of God are better known as angels. How is this kind of union possible? Why aren't there anymore of these unions between mankind and angelkind today?

These questions are what will be answered in the following chapters. What will be pointed out to begin with is the fact that these ancient men of renown, also known as giants originated at the very early stages of the earth's creation just as mankind or Homo Sapiens (more specifically the original Homo Sapiens species that modern humans called Homo Sapiens Sapiens come from) were created. This does not mean that they were made at the same time, but they do definitely appear in a close proximity timeline following the creation of Adam and Eve and the eventual spreading of mankind over the earth before the flood of Noah.

According to several geological and atmospheric studies, the earth was quite different before the time of Noah's flood. Animals (Mega Fauna) and man were larger, vegetation more lush and fertile (Mega Flora), earth's atmosphere was more peaceful, and other qualities not seen in today's world all were before the time of the great deluge. While difficult to completely map, I will attempt to form a Pangea or super continent example before it was separated into the continents we live on today to show where the species of Homo Sapien, what I have labeled Tsz-Nephilimus Sapien, and all the other extinct species of humans, originated.

In the following chapters we will explore theories and interesting evidence regarding the giant human species that I have named Tsz-Nephilimus Sapien. We will discuss the origins and migrations of them, who were their parents and future descendants, their genetic makeup and anatomy, whether they were a type of super human, and how they eventually died out, and if any of them are left even in just small samples of DNA? We will be exploring a unique idea of how other species of humanity such as Neanderthals, Homo Erectus, Homo Habilis, and so on possibly came from Homo Sapien and Tsz-Nephilimus Sapien. What this means is that it is possible all other human specimens that have been discovered in archeological digs, seen as part of our history, and had a common origin of creation from an original host or hosts.

Being compatible genetically, both God's created man and the angel/human hybrids could have produced multiple offspring that would become new species from a vast array of unique genetic offspring from pure Nephilim (Hebrew for giant and fallen) mating, Nephilim/human mating, Nephilim next generation and human mating, and so on and so forth. In short, the procreation possibilities had enough genetic material present or for the future to give rise to other human species. This will be discussed in detail in the later chapters.

It should be pointed out that the word Nephilim is controversial as the word is used to identify both giants and fallen angels. This is one of the reasons I have created a scientific name for the giants to ease the confusion. These theories and ideas have been carefully researched and outlined over a two-year study of Biblical, theological, archeological, anthropological, scientific, and medical research. It is my hope to open up a new way of seeing all the mysteries of the word of God come together with His great creation through science and discovery.

CHAPTER 2: ORIGINS

All life has a common place of origin. From this original birthing comes the future generations where a species can live, thrive, and eventually move on to new locations. With Tsz-Nephilimus Sapien, the origins can be traced all the way back to Genesis 6:1, 2, and 4. We see in those verses parental lineage, genetic code, where, and who they are in history, mythology, and legends of the world. Genesis 6:1, 2, and 4 says *"And it came to pass, when men began to multiply on the face of the earth, and daughters were born unto them, that the sons of God saw the daughters of men were fair; and they took them wives of all which they chose... There were giants in the earth in those days; and after that, when the sons of God came in unto the daughters of men, and they bore children to them, the same became mighty men which were of old, men of renown* (KJV)." These scriptures provide vast amounts of detailed knowledge for the origins of mankind. From them we can breakdown and dissect each part of the scriptures to better understand all that they contain.

In verses one and two we see the parentage of Tsz-Nephilimus Sapien. These are the sons of God and daughters of man. Another word for sons of God is angel. This part of the verse has been discussed and argued by the top educated minds the world over. It is a very complicated area to properly explore when dealing with the sexuality of angels and humans. We will look at this area in a later chapter. What can be gathered from these verses information is from the union of these two species comes a completely new species of human, or hybrid human.

The process of hybridization or the making of hybrids occurs when combining different varieties of organisms to create a hybrid. This includes hybrid making with genetics involved from heterozygous, which is breeding two genetically distinct individuals. Genetic hybrids that carry two different alleles (alternative gene forms) of the same gene, structural hybrids that have fused gametes (cells) differing with at least one chromosome made by structural abnormality. Numerical hybrids, which is the fusion of different gametes having different haploid (cells with chromosome and homologous copies) number of chromosomes, and permanent hybrid where only the heterozygous genotype occurs because any homozygous (gene with identical alleles) combinations are lethal. Hybrids can also be defined as offspring from interbreeding species.

From breeding between subspecies within a species also called intra-specific hybrids, interspecific, intergeneric and interfamilial hybrids brings new creations. Finally, crosses between populations, breeds, or cultivars (plant groups in agriculture) within a single species can create new life. This means certain individuals are selected for a trait or characteristic that is favored to breed with another selected specimen in the hopes that the traits would be passed on to the offspring.

From the brief explanation of hybridization comes a vast amount of wealth to point out where the offspring of angel/human hybrids, and God's pure mankind creation would produce. The children born from the women who had sexual relations with angels, called the *Bene-Elohim* in Hebrew, at a certain point in time were genetically compatible with the pure human or Homo-Sapiens that God had begun from His first two humans, Adam and Eve. To properly understand the terminology and taxonomy used, let us look at the words Homo Sapien and Tsz-Nephilimus Sapien.

Coined by famous zoologist and physician Carl Linnaeus, Homo Sapien comes from two Latin words. Homo comes from the root word *Hominis* meaning man or human being. Sapien is a Latin word for wise. Together they mean wise man or human. The scientific name of Nephilim, Tsz-Nephilimus Sapien, is my own original scientific term. It is derived from three places. Tsz, in honor of the first name of a friend from Hong Kong who first inspired my research. Nephilimus, derived from the Hebrew word Nephilim meaning giant. Sapien, from the Latin word for wise. Together the definition of the name means wise giant. The naming of a species is known as bionomial nomenclature, the formal system of naming a species (usually with the combining of Latin and non Latin words).

Why give a scientific name classification to the Nephilim? Because what I write about has to do with an entire species that spans both biblical and non-biblical timelines. This species shared the entire planet with God's mankind. The names that are listed in the Bible are associated with tribes and groups that the giants and the remnants of the giants made a civilization from before and after the flood of Noah. The species name however is to classify the entirety of the people both original and later generations. It is a way to show their associations with later human populations and species hence a scientific name is only appropriate when learning more about them.

The name Nephilim is an interchangeable word. Some scholars use the word to describe giants as the word means giant in one definition. Others use Nephilim to describe the Bene Elohim, as another definition of Nephilim is to fall. The identification of Nephilim with angels then has the giants identified with the word Elioud (also spelled Eljo) by some Jewish scholars. Some consider the Elioud as the sons of the Nephilim (the giants in this identification), and the next generation from the first giants. It is for this reason of multiple interchangeable words, and controversial identification between giants and angels that the name Tsz-Nephilimus Sapien will be used in identifying the species of giants alone.

As we progress in this book, I will explain a theory that states that all other human species that became extinct originated from both Tsz-Nephilimus Sapien and Homo Sapien What this means is that the original host species or host parents of the human race are God's original created man and the angel/human hybrid man. If we consider certain facts, then this could make very good sense. I should point out that there are many different theories about man's origins. Some scientists think that the first human of the genus Homo is called Homo Erectus, and Homo Sapien descended from them. Others believe that Homo Erectus and Homo Sapien are two separate species. I mention this to point out that there are many different theories and opinions about man's origins. My theory is based on my own personal study, research, and careful observation of truth, science, and fact to make my case on my theory.

Here is my theory. First, you have humans and hybrids. Obviously both groups will breed with their own respected species and have offspring. From Biblical study and observations of attraction, we can assume both species will breed together. Now, we have a third species of mankind to deal with in existence. From there, they will continue to breed with one group, then together, then another group will mate with that group and so on and so forth. If all three groups produce within their own species and with each other outside their respected species, the outcome is obvious. We will have multiple different humans that were spawned from hybrids and purebred humans with unique genetics, mutations, physical and physiological characteristics, and large to small numbers depending on the amount of each species produced.

New Species Creation Chart

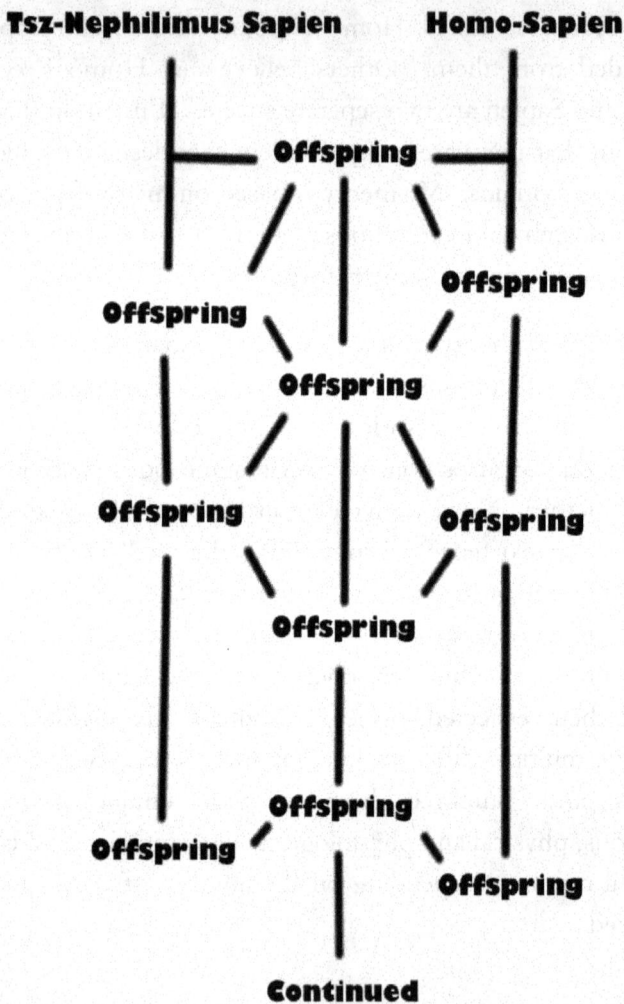

Tsz-Nephilimus Sapien   **Homo-Sapien**

Offspring

Offspring

Offspring

Offspring

Offspring

Offspring

Offspring

Offspring

Offspring

Continued

* New Species Creation Chart made by Dr. Harry Assad Salem III

The New Species Creation Chart on the previous page shows the outline of the two original species (genus or original ancestors), and how their procreation methods would intersect each other. The chart shows that each group would procreate in their own species and continue on down their respected bloodlines. Then, we see the two top Sapien species have cross species intercourse and create a whole new hybrid species. The continuing of this process would be the same with each new generation with one to multiple new human species popping up with enough genetic material to continue for several generations.

Why refer to each new generation of humans made from each union of each different original human species as an entirely new species? With each new generation arriving comes what is called Polygenic and Mendelian traits. Polygenic traits are more than one genetic locus (position of a gene or significant gene sequence on a chromosome), environmental influence on external and internal traits, and genotypes (genetic part of a cell responsible for specific characteristics of an individual) development and interactions with other organisms. Mendelian traits are one genetic locus expression not influenced by the environment. The most abundant of these traits comes from Polygenic traits.

Polygenic traits leads to Polygenic inheritance. These are traits that are influenced by more than one loci (locus) in genes. They makeup hair and skin color for example. They can't be traced to one specific gene or chromosome. Such colors that we see in skin can be governed by 3 to 6 loci and at least twelve alleles (one of a number of alternative forms of the same gene or genetic locus). These are where we get the many different people of the world today. This shows that no matter where anyone is in the world, who their parents are, or other physical traits someone has, we all come from one original past. We read in Genesis 1:28, *"And God blessed them, and God said unto them, be fruitful, and multiply, and replenish the earth, and subdue it: and have dominion over the fish of the sea, and over the fowl of the air, and over every living thing that moveth upon the earth* (KJV)."

This was written before the fall in the garden of Eden, and could very well mean that there were multiple humans already on the earth with Adam and Eve simply being the first of mankind. Going back to Genesis 6:3 we read, *"And the Lord said, My spirit shall not always strive with man, for that he also is flesh: yet his days shall be an hundred and twenty years* (KJV)." The first scripture shows that if there were other humans on the earth before the fall of mankind, then there would be enough people to populate the planet over time and multiple generations of new people coming into existence. We will explore the migration of the people of the earth in more detail later.

In the verse regarding man's flesh and age, we do see two unique bits of information presented. First, man was made of flesh. Everything that gives birth gives off unique traits that are birthed from past generations. Cells and traits that were from parents are present in their offspring. A fascinating thing about inherited traits is that if it's not present in one generation, then it could be found in another as some genes actually lie dormant until passed on into another child of the same bloodline. One example of this is when a son or daughter may not look so much like their mother or father, but look like their grand parents from either side of the family. While I have some of my parents looks, I predominately look far more like my grandfather on my father's side who my father and I are named after, Harry Assad Salem. After the flesh traits come the age factor. Man was made to live after a certain point to be only about 120 years of age. Now, early humans in the Bible lived to be way into the 800 and 900 years range. This was both before and after the flood of Noah, but ultimately began to whither down to the 120 years after a few more generations passed. Abraham, the father of the Arab and Jewish people, had a father named Terah who lived to be 205 years old. Abraham died past the age of 120 at 175. His first son, Ishmael, lived to be 137 years old before he died. The mention of these individuals is to point out that mankind aka Homo-Sapiens or Homo Sapiens Sapiens were going from 900 years old to 200 years, 175 years, 137 years, and so on until they arrive to the age groups modern humans live to be today. These two human traits prove that the earlier traits mentioned on how mankind interacts with his environment are vital to their existence and survival. While not going too deep into theories and ideas on Noah's flood; what will be pointed out is that the earth did indeed have a change in its atmosphere, which changed all the environments on the earth. This change affected mankind and completely altered what humans were, and ultimately turned them into what they are today.

In regards to Tsz-Nephilimus Sapien, or the giants as they are often called, they too possessed unique flesh features and age. Many people are not sure how old the giants could in fact, become. I have studied their physiology and will talk about the flesh of the giants later. The age factor for them was also 900 years, but could have continued way past the flood times. One giant during the time of Moses was said to be the last of his kind. His name was Og. He appears in Numbers 21:33-35, Deuteronomy 3:1-11, Psalms 135:11, Psalms 136:20.

Og was a king of a nation or city-state called Bashan. Numbers 21:33-35 reads, *"And they turned and went up by the ways of Bashan: and Og the king of Bashan went out against them, he, and all his people, to the battle at Edrei. And the Lord said unto Moses, fear him not: for I have delivered him into thy hand, and all his people, and his land; and thou shalt do to him as thou didst unto Sihon king of the Amorites, which dwelt at Heshon. So they smote him, and his sons, and all his people, until there was none left him alive: and they possessed his land (KJV)."* Deuteronomy 3:1-11 and Numbers 21:33-35 read similar to each other as they discuss the same battle with king Og. What part is most interesting though is the verse and information of Deuteronomy 3:11, *"For only Og king of Bashan remained of the remnant of giants; behold, his bedstead was a bedstead of iron; is it not in the Rabbath children of Ammon? Nine cubits was the length thereof, and four cubits the breadth of it, after the cubit of a man (KJV)."* We will discuss the height and physical features of Og later. What I will mention is the age of Og. From my research I have discovered that he may have been close to 900 years old.

Depending on further evidence, Og may be close or even over a thousand years old. If this were true then he would be older than Methuselah, who lived to be 969 years old. The reason for mentioning his and all the other Biblical characters ages is to point out that they lived for a very long time. Being individuals that had both longevity and vitality into their advanced years shows humans at one time had hundreds of years to procreate and have multiple offspring. Depending on the rate of growth, these children could then have their own long lives and continue doing what their fathers and their fathers before them did. This would give enough time to fill the earth with enough variety of humans, both different and similar, to create all the vast varieties of human species archeologists and anthropologists are always digging out of the ground around the world.

While not all are giants, the other human species such as Neanderthals, Homo Erectus, Homo Habilis, and so on display many characteristics such as large skulls, long limbs, and muscular features for increased strength that could be derived from Tsz-Nephilimus Sapien, early Homo-Sapien, and their hybrid offspring. With enough population of one generation, it should be noted that the word hybrid would no longer apply to a species, as they would have enough of their own genetic code to continue making their own species without the original host parents. This is known as speciation.

The one major setback of all these species including the giants is that at a certain point their bloodlines and compatible genetic material for procreation would become scarce or die out all together. This is known as genetic drift, which is a change in the frequency of a gene variant, or allele, in a population due to random samplings of organisms (too little or too much of parental or other genes or genetic material in the host body).

This then makes the alleles in the offspring from the parents play a game of chance in determining whether a given individual survives and reproduces. Any population allele frequencies must have enough copies or fractions of a particular gene form to ensure that a species will survive. If genetic drift occurs, then it may cause gene variants to die out completely and reduce genetic variations. I call this genetic extinction.

We will discuss the sexual relationships between mankind and angels later. I will point out that this kind of union was never supposed to happen. Two scriptures in the Old and New Testament give testament to this. In Daniel 2:43 we read, *"And whereas thou sawest iron mixed with miry clay, they shall mingle themselves with the seed of men: but they shall not cleave (hold on) one to another, even as iron is not mixed with clay* (KJV)." Then, in 1 Peter 3:18-20 it says, *"For Christ also hath once suffered for sins, the just for the unjust, that He might bring us to God, being put to death in the flesh, but quickened by the Spirit: By which also He went and preached unto the spirits in prison; Which sometime were disobedient, in the days of Noah, while the ark was preparing, wherein few, that is, eight souls were saved by water* (KJV)."

Both of these scriptures are making reference to the angels that had sex with their earthly wives, and were ultimately doomed for it as angels are not to marry or have offspring. This created a twisted nature in both the angels and their offspring. It is believed that the great evil in the world before the flood of Noah was the result of this, angel and human union, making a type of 'sins of the father being present in the children' curse that spread across the face of the earth.

Speaking of spreading across the earth, where did these giants live? Were they only living in the lands that the Bible mentions? Did they spread elsewhere before and after the flood (Genesis 6:4 does confirm that there were giants before and after the flood when the Bene Elohim came into the daughters of men to have more children)? Did they have a common place of birth only to eventually migrate to new lands? The answers to these questions will be revealed in the following chapter.

CHAPTER 3: MIGRATION AND SETTLEMENT

When we take a look at complex social structures like the ones made by humans, we understand the need of that species to move, grow, and thrive from one location to another. The need for change in humanity is a desire. To survive, man must be constantly challenged. This challenge often comes in the form of literally seeking out new horizons by traveling to new lands.

Most early human species such as Homo Sapiens were once known as hunter-gatherers. While modern humans have become predominately agricultural and pastoral (animal raising) based societies in league with industrial society, city building, and technological growth, the original need to hunt and collect food at one time the driving force of mankind. All societies have built and grown over the ages. The gathering and hunting for food, clothes, and sport was the inspiration for taking things to the next level. In today's social structure; fashion, pictures, TV shows, sports, education, food and agriculture all have been inspired by mans constant migration throughout the world. If we did not travel the world, then we would not have discovered the things that have inspired mankind to greatness.

Referring back to Romans 1:20, from the English Standard Version, we read, *"For His invisible attributes, namely His eternal power and divine nature, have been clearly perceived, ever since the creation of the world, in the things that have been made. So they are without excuse* (ESV)." The ability to be inspired and create what is found in nature is the same as in God. This is also true of God's human creation. As individuals made in the image of God, man is to be inspired to create, make, build, and grow all that we can because we share this same passion with God.

It is God's greatest desire to teach His creation in all areas of life. The Bible is full of some of the greatest accomplishments of mankind. While much of the history found in the Bible does have hardship, the end results are of accomplishment and achievement. Had the Jewish people not traveled from their roots in Ur (Iraq) throughout the areas of Asia and Africa, then they would have never grown close to God, learned to make their own culture, and become rulers of their own destiny. They also would have never had their own homeland that is today the nation of Israel.

I should go into a little bit of detail on the subject of mankind's ancestors. I have studied anthropology and archaeology for several years. In that time I have observed many different studies and sciences concerning from where mankind came. While I believe that Homo Sapiens are God's original created man, there are several other human species and alleged human species that are found to possibly be older than Homo Sapien.

Many of these other species however are not completely recognized as human species. Two sample species would be Orrorin Tugenesis and Sahelanthropus Tchadensis. They are said to have small brains, long limbs, and may or may not have been bipedal (walk on two legs). This would make them more apelike than human. I bring this up to explain that some people believe that man comes from ape. This has been an ongoing belief and disbelief struggle ever since it was first theorized. Let me be clear that man and ape are not the same species. Acts 17:26 reads *"And He made from one man every nation of mankind to live on all the face of the earth, having determined allotted periods and the boundaries of their dwelling place* (ESV)." God makes it clear when He uses the words man and mankind to point out that we are an original creation made in His image.

I accept that man and ape are members of the primate family. However, primates have two distinct lineages known as Strepsirrhines, which are suborder primates, and Haplorhines that are simians (anthropoids) and tarsiers (low class primates that live on islands in Southeast Asia). The Haplorhines order has what is called a clade. The word clade is taken from the Greek word *klados* meaning branch. Each species present today has a single branch linked to a common ancestor connected to all lineal descendants. You could call this a genetic tree of life, or a family tree. In short, apes belong to an ape genetic branch, and man to a human genetic branch.

Using genetics is the key to putting this 'ape equals man' debacle to rest. While there are many studies conducted the world over on this topic, the most basic understanding study is the percentage difference study between man and ape, or great ape as they are sometimes called. Man and ape (and monkeys for that matter) have a two to five percent difference in their DNA. This difference is defined as the removed traits in one species while found in another, and missing to non-existent traits in one species that are seen in another. Allelic polymorphisms, inactive specific genes, repetitive genomic DNA, and even effects of retroviruses are different in ape and man.

These little percentage differences prove that not only is man and ape not blood related ancestral species, but that they can't mate and produce offspring. No union of the bloodlines means no genetic branches with any common ancestry. Two scriptures correlate with this truth. Deuteronomy 23:2 says, *"No one born of a forbidden union may enter the assembly of the Lord. Even to the tenth generation, none of his descendants may enter the assembly of the Lord* (ESV)." Then, Leviticus 19:19 reads *"You shall keep my statutes. You shall not let your cattle breed with a different kind. You shall not sow your field with two kinds of seed, nor shall you wear a garment of cloth made of two kinds of material* (ESV)." God never intended mankind and animal to interbreed. This is why man and ape never could be of a common ancestral link.

Every living thing has a common genetic branch. Genesis 1:24,25 reads *And God said, Let the earth bring forth the living creature after his kind, cattle, and creeping thing, and beast of the earth after his kind: and it was so. And God made the beast of the earth after his kind, and cattle after their kind, and every thing that creepeth upon the earth after his kind: and God saw that it was good* (KJV)." Everything that God created has a common ancestor made for each of its own kind. Apes have their own original common ancestor, and mankind has its own original common ancestor that is made in God's image.

I would advocate the idea that apes could have come long before mankind. Genesis makes it clear that land animals existed before mankind. Primates of other species other than man would no doubt be included in this understanding. With this in mind, it could account for the several millions of years old skeletons of some primate species that are always being discovered and studied. Man could have arrived millions of years later while apes had already been on the earth. This makes since when put into consideration with the creation timeline mentioned in Genesis chapter one. Genesis 1:28 says, *"And God blessed them (man), and God said unto them, be fruitful and multiply, and replenish the earth, and subdue it: and have dominion over the fish of the sea, and over the foul of the air, and over every living thing that moveth upon the earth* (KJV)."

This scripture shows how it was bred into humanity to spread and multiply all over the earth. We must remember that all people of the world come from a common place of origin. Proverbs 22:28 reads *"To not move the ancient land mark that your fathers have set* (ESV)." We must remember our past because everybody everywhere comes from somewhere else. The earliest place mankind has been discovered through bodily remains and carbon dating of existence evidence is in Africa. When I first learned of this discovery, I recalled two

Biblical realizations.

The first realization I had is that mankind wasn't created in the garden of Eden like many people believe. According to Genesis 2:8, God had planted the garden of Eden eastward (the direction the Bible lists). God then placed mankind in the garden to live. The second realization is that mankind very possibly did originate in Africa. The exact location of where mankind was born in Africa is presumed to be the nation of Ethiopia. This is the location of the oldest human remains thus far recorded.

When I was a student earning my degree in anthropology, I paid considerable attention to geography. I was never very good at maps or navigating, but I paid attention to my studies because I wanted to learn all I could about a skill like map reading, because I knew it might help me as a reliable tool in the future. I especially like to study old world maps.

Studying the geography of real and hypothetical old-world maps (hypothetical in the understanding of some maps were alleged locations of places but may or may not have been accurate or proven places at all) was fascinating to me, and opened up a world of possibilities for exploration and revelation. My most favorite places to study on old world maps were ancient kingdoms and nations of the Middle East. I studied places like Ur, Mesopotamia, Chaldea, and Persia. These were the nations that birthed the modern Jewish, Arab, and other Middle East people and cultures.

When I began my research into ancient humans, I had a moment where I was taken back to those old world kingdoms. There was a thought in the back of my mind that

I thought needed checking. I remembered all the hieroglyphics, statues, and artistries of ancient Egypt. These arts portrayed all the culture, history, and people living, and who visited ancient Egypt. I remembered all over the Middle East were these same kinds of arts, statues, and writings in what is known as cuneiform that all looked similar; as if copied or identical in appearance.

These civilizations such as Mesopotamia and Chaldea were highly advanced in their times that they existed. I could make the argument that these cultures inspired future Greek and Egyptian societies. I could even surmise that some of the later people of Egypt and Greece had a few of its people descended from these Middle East and Asiatic nations. We need to realize that the earth is always changing. Continents drift and move, islands rise and sink, and landmarks appear and disappear overnight. The information given in Genesis 2:8 about man coming to live in the garden of Eden from the west to the east is believable because at the pre flood times the continents would have been much closer together.

The continents could have even been connected to each other. Various studies into geology have given proof that at one point in time all the continents formed one super continent. This super continent is called Pangea. Pangea is derived from the Greek words *pan* meaning for all, and *gaia* meaning land. The Pangea existed during the late Paleozoic and early Melozoic eras. This could very well be the way the earth's lands were before the time of the flood. It is also believed that there are other supercontinents that predate Pangea such as Rodinia (or Pangea I as it was once known) that existed during the Neoproterozoic era, and Columbia from what is identified as the Paleoproterozoic era.

Pangea Photo Courtesy of en.user:Kieff

With the continents being more closely connected, then travel and migration would be much easier for mankind. With the Pangea existing before the flood of Noah, which consisted of both great rains from the sky and volcanic eruptions from the ocean floor, then it is possible that non-continental land like land bridges and underwater mountain ranges may have been visible and crossable. In short, population growth and expansion of the human race all over the then known world was most definitely doable and made easier in the early days of the human race. This coincides perfectly with what is written in Genesis 1:28 about man being fruitful, multiplying, and filling or replenishing the earth.

If God's created man came from what would become Ethiopia, Africa, then the next question to ask is from where did the hybrids come? I want to point out one little hypothesis that I contemplated for this study. Did the hybrids appear before or after the fall of man in the garden of Eden? This is an interesting question because often times scriptures can go back and forward in time.

In Genesis 1:28, 2:24 (which talks of children leaving their parents to have their own families), and in 4:14, 15, 16, and 17 (the scriptures dealing with Cain and his descendants) we see that man multiplied and went out before the fall, that children were to grow and follow in their parents footsteps, have other children and families, and that there were other humans on the planet besides the children of Adam and Eve post fall.

There are many scholars that believe there were other human beings born before the fall of man. Some believe these other humans to be the sons and daughters of Adam and Eve ranging from about thirty-seven pre fall offspring. I believe that Adam and Eve were the very first humans that God made. He made Adam as a baby instead of a fully grown man to raise, educate, and teach knowledge so he could become the keeper of the earth that God would make Adam to be. God also made Adam as an infant to help him learn how to take care of his own children one day from infancy into adulthood. If Adam grew up from a baby into an adult, he could learn about all the bodily functions a male child would go through, understand his physiology, and then would have the knowledge to help his own children or any other humans to properly enter adulthood. The same with Eve as she was taken from Adams rib. It is very possible that both Adam and Eve grew up, though Adam slightly older as he could speak when Eve was made, to know what it was to be human, to be parents, and to be responsible adults when the time came.

The idea (if possible) of hybrids coming before the fall is complicated to explain. However, Genesis 6:2 says *"That the sons of God saw the daughters of men that they were fair (beautiful); and they took them wives of all they chose* (KJV)." When we see the word wives used, then that means that the women of the earth weren't committing any immoral acts. While the sons of God were no doubt fallen or would become fallen angels by having sexual relations with mankind; we can argue that because the daughters of men were wives that they had not themselves committed sinful acts. This would mean that they still walked in righteousness with God until the actual fall of man by Adam and Eve. This is only a hypothesis with only a handful of scriptures to work from, but it is an idea to consider.

From my research, I have deduced that Tsz-Nephilimus Sapien would have originated in Asia. Tracing the original birthplace has been difficult. Archeological, anthropological, skeletal or forensic evidence or studies that are limited to use makes for a bit of an information minefield to navigate. There have been many books and studies of Nephilim conducted, but not very many have been done on a location, or on an actual birthplace. This led me to conduct my own research into studying cartography and forensic research. From a year long study of Biblical sources, archeological sources, artistic and masonry works, and many texts and maps, I narrowed the origin spot in Asia to a place called Sumer.

SUMER, AKKAD AND ELAM

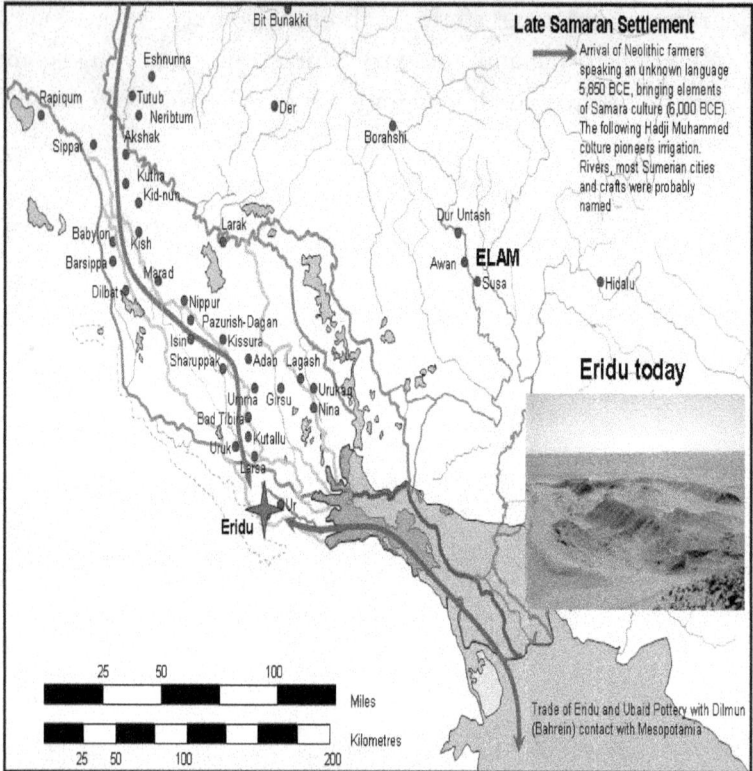

Map Courtesy of John D. Croft

Sumer is located in modern day Southern Iraq. This area includes what would (post Sumer culture) become the southern part of Mesopotamia. Permanent settlement of the area occurred between c. (circa) 5500 and 4000 BC by non-Semitic (descendants of Shem) people. The actual area however, has had many different people that had their own culture and civilizations that were of non-Sumerian people.

The timeline that I used predates all these future cultures that would be studied post flood. These people that the Tsz-Nephilimus Sapien would come from and breed with were of the earliest humans and possible descendants that would come later. Two scriptures I have that can support my claim that the hybrids came from Asia aside from when Adam was placed in Asia, where Eden was, and the people that Adams son Cain would interact with and have his descendants.

First, let us take a look at the scriptures that deal with Adam leaving the garden of Eden, or the nation of Eden. We read in Genesis 3:24, 25, *"Therefore the Lord God sent him forth from the garden of Eden, to till the ground from whence he was taken. So He drove out the man; and He placed at the east of the garden of Eden Cherubims, and a flaming sword which turned every way, to keep the way of the tree of life* (KJV)."

If we are to interpret the wording in literal terms, then Adam returned to from where he first came from. This could very well be Ethiopia. When we look at where the angels and flaming sword were placed, in the east of the garden of Eden, This could be the entrance to the whole nation of Eden's eastern borders as it says 'east of the garden.' Each word and preposition in the Bible used always represents a literal description just as technical terminology would represent exactly what is being spoken or described in technical terms.

The Bible is a masterpiece of literally work, and would thus use all grammar and vocabulary rules and words in proper fashion to correspond exact meaning or definition to not miss anything of importance and teaching. The last scripture is Genesis 4:16, *And Cain went out from the presence of the Lord, and dwelt in the land of Nod, on the east of Eden* (KJV)."

The land of Nod is believed to be where modern day Iran is located. The land however could be a much wider geographical area as both Iran and its predecessor, Persia, would have made their territorial boundaries at a much later time. The technical terms used to describe the guardian Cherubim and flaming sword east of the garden of Eden could have been placed there for the need to keep out the people of Nod. Based on the Genesis six descriptions for man being very evil, the people of Nod could have been very violent people. This would then make the security for Eden necessary not just to keep Adam and Eve out, but all of the people of Nod who were east of Eden.

Following Cain living in Nod, we know he and his descendants built many cities in many places. I believe that other humans also built up many great cities of what is called the Antediluvian or Tertiary Age. This shows that there were enough humans for the Bene-Elohim to choose wives for themselves.

The Sumer area is located beneath the territories that the nation of Eden would have been located. Had the Bene-Elohim or the sons of God selected wives from both the area of Nod and possibly the other areas from Africa like Ethiopia, then they could have taken their wives and settled, or at least procreated, in the Sumer area where the hybrid human/angel children would have originated. This could have also led to some giants being in the land of Nod and furthering the need to keep the eastern borders secure from intruders or invaders.

From the area of Sumer, Tsz-Nephilimus Sapien could have left the area, traveled to multiple locations (most likely over the entire world as time passed and evidence suggests), taken wives or mates from their own species or other Homo Sapien humans, and gave birth to the other hybrids that would eventually become extinct from the flood of Noah and the lack of enough genetic material for them to procreate and replenish their individual species. We see evidence of possible giant humans and angels all throughout the ancient lands of Sumer and surrounding areas that would make up later civilizations, nations, and empires such as Mesopotamia, Chaldea (where Babylon is) Assyria, and Persia, Egypt, China, and many other ancient and future locations. In the next chapter I will show you how to identify individual people from ancient art and masonry.

CHAPTER 4: ART & STONE

Art is based on expression. This has multiple meanings as art can represent a person, place, a people, academia, and the supernatural. Art can have several outlets for creation. It can be done on canvas, stone, medal, or even the human body with such practices as tattooing or body piercing. One area that is expressed through art is history.

In the book of Exodus, we see a book of the Bible filled with details pertaining to artistic expression. Among the scriptures in Exodus, verses 35:35 and 28:3 are most prominent in regards to art. Exodus 35:35 reads, *He has filled them with skill to do every sort of work done by an engraver or by a designer or by an embroiderer in blue and purple and scarlet yarns and fine twined linen, or by a weaver by any sort of workmen or skilled designer* (ESV)." In Exodus 28:3 we read, "*You shall speak to the skillful, whom I have filled with a spirit of skill, that they make Aaron's garments to consecrate him for my priesthood* (ESV)."

These two scriptures represent the fact that every artist has their own unique skill or skills. Being that God has given us a spirit of skill, then man's hands may often have inspiration from the spiritual realm. This proves that what we see in art from museums and books have influences from spiritual and real life.

When we look at ancient art, statues, and architecture, we see a culture's and civilization's soul frozen in time. Ancient masonry was done by the master builders and craftsmen of respected people. The scriptures we read in Exodus are representing the Jewish people who were trained to be master craftsmen in one of the greatest civilizations of the old world, ancient Egypt. Though slaves, the Hebrews were the builders of Egypt's legacy. For over four hundred and thirty years the Hebrews (an Egyptian word meaning wanderer) were building, painting, sculpting, and writing the legacy of a foreign (Egypt) people.

These learned skills would eventually be applied to the Jewish culture. I don't like the history of how Israel was at one time a people of slavery. Slavery is wrong and should always be condemned. That said, had this event not occurred, then Israel would have not acquired the knowledge they would need to forge their own cultural identity. One could look at it as a trade off from slave to master through trial and error, then trial and success. All things can have a unique destiny when it fits a purpose from God.

Egypt used two types of art forms. The first is the written

word art we see called Hieroglyphics. These writing systems were made up of hieratic, demotic, merotic, and proto-sinatic systems of what is known as lonographics that represented a concept instead of a vowel sound. The second form is called pictograph or pictogram. Pictography is roughly pure pictures for a form of writing based on resemblance to an object. Hieroglyphics are considered to be slightly pictographic, but because the writing system is based on concept rather than resemblance, that excludes it from the pictograph family. Pictographs are usually seen as picture drawings.

A system of writing called Cuniform script is a pictographic system. It uses shapes and symbols to tell stories. This system evolved into an eventual alphabetic style with consonants and vowels as the writing system became more expanded, but the original and much larger script is considered almost pure pictoral representation. When looking at pictographs and lonographs, we see a type of ancient reality show.

What we read and look at carved and painted on walls is ancient drama with surprise twists and outcomes that have a seasonal ending. Civilizations fade from history. The only thing that is certain is that there are always shadows of people in future generations. An appropriate old Arabic saying is 'different name, same land, and same people.' Egypt has hieroglyphics of large men and women who were of both native and foreign people. Many of them are of a race of people the Egyptians called the Tammahu. The Tammahu were believed to be very tall people from the lands around Egypt.

When we look into art concerning giant people, the best pictographs come from ancient Sumer and the surrounding countries. These other countries include Mesopotamia, Chaldea, Assyria, Persia, Greece, the early kingdoms of India and China, and various nomadic tribes such as the Scythians and Tocharians. The art of these people portrays two very unique figures. The first is of men of great physical stature (height) and strength. The second is certain individuals with divine or supernatural attributes.

To make portraits or renditions of characters for paintings and statues, typically real life models are used. These models tend to look exactly like the images that they are portraying. What this means is that not all people used for modeling are representing themselves, but are inspiring the artist to make what they are creating look like the models without being the real life version of them.

Modern video game designers and comic book artists follow the same pattern. They keep their inspired characters as closely to life like to the original model as possible. While a stretch, it can be very likely that many ancient world artists and sculptors had actual Tsz-Nephilimus Sapiens or descendants pose as models. One way to possibly prove this idea is with the portrait of a Sumerian king named Gilgamesh.

As a kid I enjoyed reading DC and Marvel comics. I loved one particular show called Batman the Animated Series. In one episode they had a man called Bane as the villain. In the episode Batman investigated Bane and discovered that Bane had gained his strength and size from a project in prison called Project Gilgamesh. Batman's butler Alfred then made the comment that Gilgamesh was named after a warrior to which Batman corrected Alfred and said it was named after the ultimate warrior. I found that statement very interesting. When I got older I read what is called the *Epic of Gilgamesh*. The story was quite fascinating and definitely showed it was not an exaggeration when batman called Gilgamesh the ultimate warrior.

Gilgamesh, originally pronounced Bilgamesh, was a Sumerian king that ruled between 2800 and 2500 BC. He was the king of an ancient city called Uruk (Biblical Erech) for 126 years. He was later worshipped as a demi god in history, and many of his exploits have been chronicled in various mythologies. What is known about him that is of particular interest is his mention in Sumerian poetry, which predates the Akkadian poetry that mentions him in more detail.

Gilgamesh has a fascinating physical appearance. He was extremely strong, considered to possess superhuman strength. He was seen as a giant in physical appearance. His statue and artistic portrayals show a man of incredible size, physical appearance similar to a modern day body builder, long hair and beard with a penetrating gaze. In my opinion, the gaze of Gilgamesh was similar to that of a soldier who had been in combat, acquired the thousand yards stare, and who knew the horrors and trials of war. This would only add to the description of Gilgamesh as the ultimate warrior.

Gilgamesh is mentioned in the Hebrew Qumran scroll called the *Book of Giants*, which is a part of the *Dead Sea Scrolls*, as a giant of the Antediluvian (pre-flood) Age. This part is skeptical as there are those that say Gilgamesh was a post flood king. What is known about him though is he was a king that was from the Sumerian area, was considered an actual king of incredible strength and size, and whose burial site may be buried under the Euphrates River that passed the city of Uruk (possibly discovered in 2003, but is still not completely believed to be his tomb for certain until further study is done on the area and more excavations are undertaken).

* Gilgamesh Courtesy of the Louvre Museum in Paris, France

When looking at the statue portrait of Gilgamesh, we often see his arms holding a lion. Originally this was thought to be a lion cub, but this is a mistake. Being a king from the continent of Asia, the lion that Gilgamesh holds would no doubt be an Asiatic lion. Asiatic lion cubs do not have manes, and do not grow them until adulthood, which is around two to three years of age; and either full to partial body length growth. These lions are slightly smaller than their African cousins, but not by much.

A typical male African lion can reach a total length of 11 feet, and an Asiatic male can reach a maximum of 9 feet. The weight of a male Asiatic lion is between 300 to 500 lbs. Depending on the actual length of the lion, we can estimate that Gilgamesh was at least past nine feet in length himself. I would estimate that based on the size of the lion being at least no more than seven to eight feet long (from another portrait I viewed with a man of about six feet standing toe to toe with Gilgamesh for size comparability), I would say that Gilgamesh stood between fourteen and fifteen feet in height. In truth, I would not be surprised if Gilgamesh was even taller than my estimates.

Amos 2:9 reads, *"Yet I destroyed the Amorites before them, though they were tall as the cedars and strong as the oaks, I destroyed their fruit above and their roots below (NIV)."* This scripture, which we will discuss in further detail in the following chapters, talks about the Amorites. The Amorites were a people from Syria and Mesopotamia, and who established the city of Babylon that would later be conquered by several other empires. They are referenced in Sumerian and Akkadian texts. The mention of the Amorites in Amos 2:9 says that they were a people as tall as cedar trees. The region that Amos 2:9 talks about would be the area of Israel, Lebanon, and Syria.

The type of cedar that would be found in this area would be Lebanon, Turkish (Taurus), Atlas (also considered Lebanon), and Cyprus Cedar. Both Lebanon and Turkish types of cedar are subspecies of trees that belong to the tree genus Cedrus Libani. The height of both of these trees can be a maximum of 40 meters, which is 130 feet tall with a trunk of 2.5 meters or 8 feet 2 inches. Though not saying that the Amorites were 130 feet tall, the point of this scripture is that the Amorites were described as very tall and very strong people.

Using this scripture and the size comparisons of the statue, Gilgamesh could very well have been a giant passed ten feet tall. Called bas-reliefs (meaning the sculptural technique used), the statues of Gilgamesh, ancient kings, angelic beings, gods, kings and other individuals all have one other unique feature. Many of the bas-reliefs have men and women of what I consider normal size height. Certain figures however, portray a much larger individual that stands well above the other people in the pictures or carvings. This style of sizing up individuals is copied in Mesopotamian, Chaldean, Assyrian, Persian, and even Egyptian and other less known civilizations.

The art of Sumerian and pre-existing cultures that came before was the inspiration for the Tigris-Euphrates Valley civilizations. The beginnings of who brought the writing systems and masonry skills to the area are unknown. Some speculate that the discoveries occurred about the same time as Egypt and the Nile Valleys early civilizations discoveries (beginnings). This would be between 5,000 and 3,000 B.C. This time period was the ending of the Stone Age as copper had been discovered in what is known as the Neolithic Age, and Aenolithic Age. The Sumerian territory was a very rich area in agriculture and trade. What it lacked however was building materials such as trees and quality stone.

Brick use, both baked and unbaked, was the building material of choice for architecture and artistry as well as some imported stone supplies when available. The Sumerians and other cultures living in the surrounding areas became master masons of stone carvings and architecture. Careful attention to detail was given for each project. Being that many of the designs represented kings and deities made the work of the artists all the more imperative to stay as close to perfect as possible. This practice of master sculpting, building, and design would be picked up by other civilizations of Greek, Aegean, Russian (Slavic), Chinese, and other Asiatic countries throughout history.

In Greek culture, we see statues and paintings of giant men of incredible strength and size. One of the biggest statues and portraits is that of the demigod Heracles or Hercules (Roman name). Heracles is considered the greatest of the ancient Greek heroes. He was the son of the chief Greek god Zeus, was half human and half divine, and possessed incredible strength and abilities. His physical appearance in portrayal has him looking like a modern day bodybuilder. In one of the greatest of ancient Greek city-states called Sparta, the Spartans used to claim that they were descended from Heracles. The warrior culture and desire to keep only the purest of human specimens (which involved inhumane pursuits of perfection such as tossing those considered unfit, runts, and handicapped from cliffs after a newborn inspection) for the state is perhaps inspired by the physical attributes of Heracles and his near perfect physical qualities.

The size and strength factors of Heracles in portrayal are what are of interest. He was said to be 15 feet tall and his strength was equal to the Titans. One of Heracles epic twelve labors involved him having to match the Titan Atlas' strength to hold the sky up that Atlas was condemned to hold up, which Heracles did with ease.

Heracles statue, courtesy of photographer Yair Haklai

Once again the possibility of an actual model looking or being the actual Heracles could be made. Heracles was not a model, but I would wager some sculptor saw him and was inspired to carve his image out of stone. Busts, images, and inspired art of Heracles can be seen in Greece, Iran, Egypt, India, and even as far as Japan (Nio guardian deities of Japan Buddhist temples are said to be inspired by Heracles). Detail to realism would have to be done with someone of the actual look and feel of someone in top physical condition.

I have studied the ancient human body and have developed a study of how such a body design would come about from certain suppressed genes and proteins that make modern humans look as they do, and how they would have looked when they were active. In ancient people these genes and proteins, if not active, would possibly give the physiques that we see in statues and portraits of ancient heroes. This type of portrayal of specific body types and unique physical features can be seen in paintings and petroglyphs from around the world. In the next chapter we will explore this kind of artwork, stonework, and metalwork in more detail.

CHAPTER 5: PILLARS AND GOLD

In 2 Chronicles 2:14 we read, "*The son of a woman of the daughters of Dan, and his father was a man of Tyre. He is trained to work in gold, silver, bronze, iron, stone, and wood, and in purple, blue, and crimson fabrics and fine linen, and to do all sorts of engravings and execute any design that may be assigned him, with your craftsmen of my lord, David your father* (ESV)." The city of Tyre is found in the nation of Lebanon. Meaning rock in its definition, Tyre is home to the legendary woman Europa that Europe was named after, Elissa who was the first queen of Carthage (the center of modern day Tunisia), and is home to many ancient sites such as the Hippodrome (horse and chariot track) that is a world heritage site.

Tyre is a heavily fortified city with great sized walls, production of an expensive purple dye called Tyrian dye that was used by royalty and nobility, and was where Jesus and the Apostle Paul preached and spent time teaching disciples. As read in 2 Chronicles 2:14, Tyre is home to great metallurgists and artists. From Tyre came the builders for the Israelite kings David and Solomon. 2 Samuel 5:11 reads, *And Hiram king of Tyre sent messengers to David, and cedar trees, also carpenters and masons who built David a house* (ESV)." Lebanon is very rich in natural resources. It is famous for its builders, carpenters, and metal workers. Next to Tyre in Lebanese history for building is Baalbek. Located in northern Lebanon, Baalbek is home to some of the most beautiful ruins of the ancient world. Among the ancient wonders of Baalbek are the monoliths, or stone monuments and pillars. These monoliths predate any of the known civilizations they settled in Lebanon. The idea behind their creation is that the size of the stones was necessary for individuals of very large height.

Baalbek and Tyre share many architectural similarities. The European connections these two cities share are another connecting factor. The cities share a migration pattern of Asiatic people to Europe. In the history of Asia, there have been many different people coming to Europe. Many also settled in Africa, which is evidenced by remains found in Egypt and other North African countries. But, a great number of people from Asia had settled predominately in Europe. Returning to the architecture, the building of such large cities and monoliths is identified as Cyclopean masonry.

The term Cyclopean masonry comes from the Greek word for the mythological one-eyed creature called the Cyclops. The definition for Cyclopean masonry is to identify mason work done with large stones for building materials. The most identifiable evidence of Cyclopean masonry is located on the Greek island of Crete. The island has similar structures to Tyre and Baalbek. Other locations with Cyclopean masonry are found in the multiple cities of Mycenae and Tiryns (both were settlements and fortress structures).

The use of Cyclopean masonry was believed to only be able to be performed by ancient Cyclopes because of the strength it would require to move the stones and boulders that made up the walls and buildings built. While Cyclopes are mythological creatures, their mention in the mason skillset was termed by a world famous philosopher. The great Greek philosopher Aristotle attributed the belief of Cyclopes carrying out the masonry as he thought they were the inventors of masonry towers and structures. While perhaps speaking in a joking or allegorical manner, it was Aristotle who coined the term Cyclopean masonry.

Tyre and Baalbek have Cyclopean mason architecture by way of the large stonework of these cities. The only difference between these Lebanese and Greek cities is that the architecture in Tyre and Baalbek are identified with much older civilizations. Greek and Roman civilizations lived and built in these cities, but there is archaeological evidence to support the sites being inhabited by older civilizations.

The importance of discussing the Cyclopean masonry in the Middle East and Europe is because the need to point out who built them. The areas of the Middle East as a whole contain many cities and city-states that have Cyclopean masonry. Another type of masonry that is seen in these areas is called Ashlar masonry. This masonry has some stonework similar to Cyclopean masonry by way of large sized stones finely shaped and squared with near perfect design.

Ashlar masonry is a more commonly practiced form of masonry. From the Latin word axilla (a diminutive form of the word axis) for plank, Ashlar masonry adheres to the phrase 'cut to perfection.' The stones of Ashlar masonry are cut to the finest unit of cuboid that is squared or cut and shaped to a design specific to the construction projects needs. Unlike rubble masonry, which is irregular shaped stones put into place with no specific order, Ashlar stones are perfected to a T in design and placement. Ashlar masonry is used in ancient and modern times. We see it in ruins from the Inca Empire, Greece, Crete, and in modern buildings throughout the United States among other places. Ashlar and Cyclopean masonry are seen together in many ruins around the world, but there are differences when compared.

Cyclopean masonry is not very refined like Ashlar. The designs are not very complex as the stone faces are often roughly hammer dressed, unworked boulders fitted together in a rough type setting. Some Cyclopean stones are seen with a level of refinement seen from some fine hammering and certain gaps in between some walls and structures where limestone is placed in chunks to give a basic tasteful design. The more refined masonry work seen throughout the world would be identified with the later civilizations living in the area at the times certain structures were built. Although many people that descended from Tsz-Nephilimus Sapien and other human species were not all highly sophisticated societies, we can surmise that some did become an advanced people that could build great civilizations or intertwined with other advanced cultures.

Returning to Egypt, there are hieroglyphics of large men, perhaps slaves or average laborers who helped build many of the great structures that made up the old and new kingdoms. In Sumer, Mesopotamia, Chaldea, and Persia there are arts and architecture that are possibly inspired or built by giants. Further to the east in China and Indo-China territory ruins of large pyramids, burial mounds, caves with amazing art and stone masonry, palaces, and cities that are quite different from traditional Chinese designs that we often see in the history of the region. Another source of evidence for Tsz-Nephilimus Sapien and their offspring descendants is seen in medal works of bronze and other metallic artistry.

I am not advocating that we see an extinct species walking around as a hidden race or a conspiracy has been done to cover up such ideas. Rather, I am saying that thousands of years after the extinction of certain human species we have at the very least seen descendants that do carry some of the genetics of certain species to an extent that we can see them throughout modern history as the last remnants of a died out race or last of their kind. The people I am about to mention are among some of the people I strongly believe carried genetic traces through what is called genetic drift from one generation to generation. Even a small trace of a Tsz-Nephilimus Sapien bloodline can be enough to at least give some modern humans their physical traits and attributes.

Going into the metal works of cultures brings the art found in iron, bronze, silver, and gold. One unique culture that produced lifestyle imagery in their metal works is the Scythians. We see a mention of the Scythians in Colossians 3:11. Colossians 3:11 reads, *"Where there is neither Greek nor Jew, circumcision nor uncircumcision, Barbarian, Scythian, bound nor free: but Christ is all, and in all* (KJV)." This scripture mentions the Scythians by name and identifies them separate from the term Barbarians. This use of the separate identity of the Scythians from other Barbarian people, which the Scythians are often identified with in other histories, is important when being identified with the Greek culture that has a deep rooted history with the Scythians.

1 Corinthians 12:13 says, *"For by one Spirit are we all baptized into one body, whether we be Jews or Gentiles, whether we be bond or free; and have been all made to drink into one Spirit* (KJV)." Both the Colossians 3:11 and 1 Corinthians 12:13 scriptures come from the same author, the Apostle Paul. These two verses were part of two letters sent by Paul to the Roman city of Corinth, and the Greek and Roman city of Colosse. It is the Greek roots of Colosse that we will take special note of in regards to the separation of Scythian and barbarian identification.

In Greek history, the Scythians were a fierce people. Originating from Indo-Iranian territory (as a separate people from the ancestors of modern day Kurdish and Persian people). The Scythians dominated southern Russia and Crimea during the 8th and 3rd centuries BCE. Coming from Central Asia, the Scythians dominated the lands from Danube to Ukraine for over four hundred years. The Scythians were horsemen like the Huns and Mongols. They are believed to be the inspiration for the legendary Centaurs (half-man, half-horse) in Greek mythology due to the terror they put into the ancient Greeks. The Scythians struck fear into both the Greeks and Persians because of their exploits. The Greek historian Herodotus wrote about their culture in his histories.

Herodotus records that the Scythians were violent people by examples seen in their burial and execution customs. This is seen by way of funeral practices involving human sacrifice to honor their dead, and rituals involving heavy drug use. Before the Romans took up the practice, the Scythians practiced crucifixion as a means of execution for punishment because of its forms of obscene and utterly offensive displays.

The Biblical prophet Jeremiah may have had a vision of the Scythians in his prophecies. Jeremiah 50:41-42 reads, *"Behold, a people shall come from the north, and a great nation, and many kings shall be raised up from the coasts of the earth. They shall hold the bow and the lance: their voice shall roar like the sea, and they shall ride upon horses, everyone put in array, like a man to the battle, against thee, O daughter of Babylon* (KJV)." The Scythians were no doubt ruthless warriors. They also possessed a sophisticated culture and society.

The Scythians were amazing artists by way of tattooing and metalworking. They were heavy into the art of tattooing. Men and women both received tattoos usually throughout the body. This practice would be carried on in later generations. Aside from tattooing, the most beautiful of the Scythians artistic skill sets was goldsmithing. Scythians worked well in decorative art. Crafting predominately in jewelry, Scythians made excellent gold pieces. Many of the Scythian pieces were designed to look like horses, Pegasus' (winged horses), deities, and riders on horseback in battle depictions. The Greeks followed Scythian battle designs in their own goldsmithing. The Greeks occasionally would present gold pieces as gifts to Scythian chiefs and political leaders. One particular piece the Greeks gave to a Scythian chief was a gold comb with a battle depiction adorning the top of it.

*Greek gold comb depiction of Scythians in battle Courtesy of Maqs

The combs depiction, made from around the late 5th to early 4th century BCE, provides an interesting look at the size of the Scythians. The figures on the comb, both on foot and horseback, show very tall and very strong men. We can measure the size of the men better by first sizing the height and length of the horse that was being rode.

Looking closer at Scythian history, we see a society of great horsemen and horsewomen. Scythian women were often equal to men and fought along side the men in battle. In the history of Asia and the areas of the steppes (eco regions of grasslands, savannahs, and prairies), we see several breeds of horses. Many of these horse breeds are extinct today while some have been able to survive and thrive. Like modern Arabs, the nations and nomadic tribes of the ancient world valued the horse as a prized possession. The Scythians as a horse-based culture valued the horse above all other possessions to the point that when a Scythian died, then their horse was buried with them. The horse was not slaughtered, but rather ceremoniously sacrificed and buried with its owner or owners. Many remains of the horses buried with their masters have been found in Scythian tombs.

From the remains discovered in Pazyryk (located in Siberia), evidence was shown that Scythians raised thoroughbreds. Thoroughbred is defined as a distinct breed of horse. A thoroughbred is sometimes referenced with purebred, which is a term for any horse (or another animal) that derives from a single breed line.

Scythians used fleet-footed (fast moving), sometimes smaller breeds of horse for warfare. However, the smaller breed of horse would be the size of the mares, which averaged about 13 hands (measurements used for horses), which is four feet and four inches tall. The mares are believed to be the horses used for the women riders, and some male riders. The size of the mares would be about the correct height for a woman rider as Scythian women were usually small with the tallest height being about five feet tall, to five feet and six inches max. The men however, were of much different height and weight. Depending on the breed of horse used due to the need of speed, endurance, and strength for carrying armaments, armor, and rider's weight, many Scythian male warriors needed larger height and length sized horses.

Scythian society had class-based systems. We see two sets of classes seen in Altai (in East-Central Asia) graves used in burial practices for upper class and common class. Common class Scythians were small people of average height about five feet and four inches. Upper class Scythians though were much taller, and much stronger. These men are described as having powerful bodies with well-built muscles and strength. Their height was also different. Many of the men had heights over six feet tall with even larger specimens. Many of these men would no doubt be the warriors that struck fear into Greek and Persian hearts.

For a man over six feet tall, the horse would have to be at least close to six feet, or sixteen to seventeen hands in height. Among the horses of the areas the Scythians occupied were two species that were perhaps the preferred choice for riding and warfare. These two horses were the now extinct Nisean horse, and the Akhal-Teke horse. The Nisean horse was used predominately by the Persian Empire. The Nisean horse was around seventeen hands or five feet and eight inches tall. The length was around eight feet, which is the same length for almost all horses. A few other Niseans are possibly close to six feet tall depending on the breeding. Niseans are described by historical analysis as having robust heads, being tall, swift, well built, and able to pull a chariot. The Nisean was considered to be an excellent warhorse. It is speculated that the Nisean horse, based on its characteristics, might have been a descendant of an original wild horse breed called the Forest horse (not to be confused with the modern day Forest horse found in Germany). The Scythians possibly had a few of these Nisean horses in their possession. The most common horse that was used by the Scythians though would more likely be the Akhal-Teke horse.

Standing at between 14 and 16 hands high, the Ahkal-Teke was (and still is) a magnificent horse. Almost three thousand years old, the breed was a staple of Scythian culture. Named after the Teke tribe of the Akhal Oasis (between Turkmenistan and Iran), the Akhal-Teke was a horse described as a magnificent beauty. The Akhal-Teke is described as having good endurance, fast legs, and possessing an amazing strength.

In 1935 when Joseph Stalin controlled the Soviet Union, a group of Akhal-Teke horses were brought to Moscow by private owners to show the amazing strength of the horse to Stalin in the hopes of being allowed to continue breeding the horse. This was due to many of the horses being confiscated by the Soviets from their owners and sent to state owned stud farms where many of them where slaughtered for food leading many breeders to flee with their prized horses. Stalin was so impressed that the owners were allowed to continue their work with the Soviet Union's backing.

The Akhal-Teke were bred with as close to pure bloodlines as possible by the Scythians. Extreme physical isolation, strong traditional senses, and the need to breed a strong war mount was the drive of the Scythians when making a Scythian horse. Like Arab Bedouins, the nomadic traditions of the Scythians kept a close eye on their prized horses to ensure a perfect specimen. The Akhal-Teke horse had strong legs, a slender but strong frame, and a high set neck. While the Scythians used the Akhal-Teke horse and possibly the Nisean horse as their primary breed of choice, they did use other horses that were native to the lands they occupied. These two horses are the ones that are seen in the graves and historical evidence of the Scythians.

The Scythians kept in their horse stocks the Mongolian or Prezwalski's horse, which is a personal favorite of mine. The Prezwalski's horse is the last of the pure wild horses in existence. It has never been tamed or ridden by modern man. I can only speculate, but I think that the Scythians, with their horse techniques, may have been able to tame them for riding. If not riding, then at least for the possibility of breeding. There have been successful crossbreeding of the Preezwalski's wild horse and other domesticated horses in modern times, and most of them were considered to be fertile hybrids (meaning the offspring could procreate with other horses in the future).

The sizes of these horses are important when determining the size of the riders. Looking back at the picture of the gold comb with rider and horse, there are two things to point out. The comb was crafted by Greek goldsmiths, and gives rise to the notion that they saw the Scythians as giants on horseback. The second is that the Greeks were only one group to make art with the Scythians as giants. The Persians and Scythians themselves have carved, designed, and drawn art of their own with Scythians (and some Persians) on horseback with heights that go past the usual size of an average rider on horseback.

When I ride a horse, my feet can slightly go past the horse's stomach. I stand at a maximum height of 6'3. When you look at both the Greek comb and other art from Persian and Scythian men on horseback, many of their renderings reveals men whose legs go past the horse's stomach. Their knees are what end at the horse's stomach. Looking at a Scythian on a horse that at a max would be between five and six feet tall with legs extending past the stomach, then we can estimate a good two to three feet from Scythian leg to pelvic region. This would put the Scythian horsemen we see in certain pieces of art at about seven, maybe even eight feet in height. The heights can vary, as we don't have an exact height reference. We can assume however, that the Scythians did have a sizeable figure for some of their mounts (horses).

I have studied and examined Greek, Persian, and Scythian art. All three cultures have Scythian horsemen with a size of at least six feet for the smallest riders, and the tallest at the seven to eight feet height for the tallest riders. While not all are giant riders, the revelation of many riders as giants on horseback helps support the belief that the Scythians do have a possible ancestry connection to Tsz-Nephlimus Sapien and their descendants. The other cultures of Greece and Persia also share some ancestry as we can see throughout their art showing these culture's people who are not of Scythian blood.

China has history that contains accounts of giants among their many dynasties. During the Ming Dynasty, which ruled from 1368 to 1644 AD, many reports of giant men of at least 15 feet tall were seen in 1555 as palace guards and archers for the emperor Zhu Houcong, or the Jiajing Emperor as he was referred to in official title. These giant soldiers were also seen being used in 1627 by either Zhu Youxiao or Tianqi Emperor who died in the same year at the age of 21, the Zhu Youjian or Chongzhen Emperor who reigned until the end of the Ming Dynasty in 1644, or both since their reigns were so close. However, the Chongzhen Emperor possibly ended the lives of the 500 (the alleged number of giants) Chinese giant soldiers, or discharged them as the emperor had undertaken the task of reforming the military by executing top military officials and field commanders he suspected were plotting against him, and/or possibly due to an empty treasury that would leave him with a need to cut back on military personnel due to budget.

These accounts of Chinese giant soldiers may also have been the inspiration behind the tomb guards in Nanjing. Ming tombs in Nanjing, China had at one time many large statues that were dressed in armor, carried swords, and were between 12 to 15 feet tall. These statues and Ming tombs in Nanjing and surrounding areas were either damaged or destroyed during the 1850-1864 Taiping Rebellion, the 1966 Cultural Revolution, and possibly from damage during the Chinese and Japanese conflicts in World War II (many massacres and bombings had occurred in Nanjing).

The tombs today are Chinese heritage sites that many people visit near Beijing and Liaoning provinces. The Chinese were known to use life size models for their military statues. The Terracotta Army of Qin Shi Huang, the first emperor of China are all life sized. Due to possible Hellenistic sculpting influence like the Terracotta statues and possible repeat styles adopted by the Ming Dynasty, then it may be possible the tomb statues are life-sized renditions (this theory is only speculative of course, but still fascinating to consider). A fascinating observation to be seen in Chinese Mandarin (Mainland China, Taiwan, and Hong Kong) is the word Nephilim (pronounced either wei da de ren or wei ren) means 'great man' when translated, which carries the same meaning as mighty man or men, stature (also identified with great by definition) and renown.

* Photo by John Thompson from Illustrations of China and its People 1873-74

Everywhere in the world has some stories and history to point out on giant humans living, working, and fighting. Referring back to the Scythians, the reason I use the species name Tsz-Nephilimus Sapien to identify the ancestors of the

Scythians is because the species is identified by multiple names. The Bible uses the term Nephilim, Rephaim, Anakim, Zamzzumims, Gibborim, Elioud and other tribes that inhabited the land of Canaan. The word Nephilim has also been used as the name of the Bene Elohim who fathered the giants. Other nations and cultures the world over also used different names for these real life giants. Therefore I use a scientific species name to label all people that made up the giants (not the angels) of old.

With the understanding that each previously mentioned cultures and civilizations have displayed giant humans in their art, that their large ruins that would possibly require exceptionally strong people to help move and build, and that the giants are indigenous to multiple areas instead of a single region of the earth leads to the next questions.

- How did they get here?

- Where did they go?

- What did they look like?

- What was their physical traits?

- What was their anatomy like?

These questions can best be answered by studying the lineages, bloodlines, and genetics of Tsz-Nephilimus Sapien.

CHAPTER 6: GENETICS & ANATOMY

The human genome is the basis of all human life. Be it ancient or modern times, all humanity would not exist without the genome that makes up our genetics. The genome consists of the DNA (deoxyribonucleic acid) that makes each individual human unique. This includes the genes and non-coding sequences (non-protein sequences) that make up the structure of DNA.

Ancient human beings were individuals of extraordinary size and strength because of what made up their genomes, or genetic material. One such study to show how this actually works was done with a strength competition and comparison. The idea was based upon who would win at arm wrestling between a Neanderthal woman and a reigning male world arm wrestling champion. The results showed that the Neanderthal woman would win. The result basis of the contest was that, while depending on certain circumstances such as training and overall strength of each individual for competition, an average Neanderthal woman has ten percent more muscle and cortical bone (osseous tissue that form bones and regulate bones main functions) levels than a modern male.

The cortical bone provides lever movement or flexibility of limbs, support for the whole body, and regulates the chemical elements released in the body. This would include the levels of cortisol (a natural steroid hormone produced in humans via the adrenal gland) that regulate muscle and strength growth. Neanderthal women also have a stronger wrist than modern humans, which would play into the woman's favor of beating the male arm wrestling champion. This observation of a Neanderthal woman versus a modern champion arm wrestler shows how powerful many ancient human species were in their respected times.

I have always strived to be a man of great health and strength. Since I was fifteen I have been what is called a gym rat. A gym rat is someone who is in a gym almost all the time, and almost never misses a day of working out. My best experience in the gym happened when I went down from 245 lbs. to 188 lbs. I went up to 205 lbs. after I packed on 16 pounds of muscle. I wanted to look like a bodybuilder, but have the strength of a power lifter. I have achieved this feat through hard work, research into how to get stronger and healthier, and by studying the human body and supplements religiously. My own merits were the result of determination and training.

When I think about ancient humans, my workout routines would be like child's play to them. I have an expression I use in the gym. I say that I train to lift 300 lbs., but giants train to lift 600 lbs. This is because from their descriptions, the giants and their descendants could lift an average weight of 300 lbs. without ever having to pick up a training weight.

Looking into the history of ancient humans has opened my eyes to many revelations. The first and foremost fact I learned is that the first humans were far different than humans of today. With each generation following natural and manmade changes in the earth's ecology would no doubt bring an 'adapt to survive' change in each new human generations.

While the Bible doesn't use specific scientific terminology, there is sufficient material for basic genetic research throughout the sixty-six books and their verses. 1 Corinthians 15:39 reads, "*For all flesh is the same, but there is one kind for humans, another for animals, another for birds, and another for fish* (ESV)." This scripture entails genetic identification, or I.D. We can gather genetic markers that can be seen in DNA testing from genetic identifications.

Acts 17:26 says, "*And He made from one man every nation of mankind to live on all the face of the earth, having determined allotted periods and the boundaries of their dwelling place* (ESV)." Referring to Adam in the scripture, we see the literal formation of a genetic family tree. In the case of Adam, we see the lineage trace of the entire human race going all the way back to the patriarch of mankind. Adam was the first man, whom the first woman came from (Eve came from his rib), then the first woman gave birth to the next generation of humans, and so forth. Adam could also be called Homo Sapien Original.

There are many factors that go into reading Biblical scriptures. Scriptures regarding the early days of earth, Adam, and all other subjects are best read in three ways. I study the scriptures in these three ways as they appear to be the most effective analytical methods to properly understand the scriptures. These three ways are the literal, or direct form according to proper meaning. The technical (also considered a form of Jargon speech), which is used in context that may have differences or be interpreted differently than what is being presented. Finally, the theoretical. The theoretical provides framework for observation and assumption of a person, place, thing, time, and/or event leading to multiple ideas of what is actually being presented in scripture.

Looking at the literal wording of scriptures used before the flood of Noah gives us the first word to describe Tsz-Nephilimus Sapien. That word is giant. The ancient world is full of stories and myths regarding and laying claim to giants. The Biblical scriptures give us the most continuous accounts of giants before and after the flood. The word giant is not a simple definition with a singular definition. There are two definitions of noun and adjective explanation for giants that are the most common.

The noun definition is an imaginary or mythical being of human form but superhuman in size. The adjective definition is of great size or force; gigantic. The word giant is not a simple definition with a singular explanation. There are two simple definitions of noun and adjective origins. Other definitions of the word giant is seen in many scientific, medical, and esoteric studies. We will be studying the medical and scientific definitions of what a Tsz-Nephilimus Sapien giant is, their physical form and attributes, abnormalities, and lifespan. As stated in the previous definitions, giants are human looking but with superhuman size, gigantic, and of great size. The gigantic size is placed into four categories. They are height, width and length, weight or mass, and physiological strength. We will break down the categories in the following chapters beginning with height.

CHAPTER 7: HEIGHT

All giants are tall. This simple statement describes what everybody thinks when they hear the word giant. Height is used to indicate how tall something is, or how high up it is. Tsz-Nephilimus Sapien is measured with height from environmental adaption and hereditary traits by means of genetic and protein synthesis and suppressing.

Proper measurement of height is essential when studying Tsz-Nephilimus Sapien. Every giant mentioned in the Bible be it a person, people (or tribe), or race all have different heights that vary from time and place. It should be noted that many actual heights are given in the various books of the

Bible, but ancient measurements are debatable based on the measurements being done with the cubit.

The cubit is an ancient unit of measurement that was used in the cultures of Israel, Egypt, and Babylon among others. The units of measurement vary from short to long inches depending on what the cubit is being used to measure. Careful exact measurement of the cubit has been conducted to aid the research of ancient giants proper sizes. To this effect the field of anthropometry is applied for height measurement. Anthropometry refers to the measurement of the human individual. Exact measurement is a link in the chain for our Biblical giants that in turn will connect to our other areas of study.

To understand the heights of ancient human species, we must have a basic knowledge of the human bodily systems that produce growth in muscle and bone. We must also have a grasp of early atmospheric conditions and environments. To understand how the anatomical traits of humans interacted with the environmental aspects of the earth will help to unlock the science of what man once was by divine creation, but ultimately suppressed by nature.

Our world has evolved with the passage of time. Animals, plants, microscopic organisms, and humans have all come and gone. Some have lived and flourished for millions of years, while others have had a lifespan that lasted for just a few seconds to minutes. The biosphere (sum of all ecosystems) that we call planet earth gives testament to God's great and delicate creation.

Hebrews 11:3 says, *"By faith, we understand that the universe was created by the word of God, so that what is seen was not made out of the things that are visible* (ESV)." Not all things can be explained simply by looking at what is visible. We must also study the things that can't be seen by the naked eye. In the case of giants, the invisible would be found in the human endocrine system.

All growth for humans begins in the endocrine system. The endocrine system is a collection of hormone-producing glands and cells located in various parts throughout the body. This system includes the pituitary gland, adrenal glands, thyroid and parathyroid glands, and the pancreas. Bone and general growth are controlled by the pituitary gland. The pituitary gland is also called the master gland. The pituitary gland controls growth hormone or GH. Growth hormone works throughout the whole body to promote protein synthesis. Growth hormone is vital for normal growth and development. The growth hormone in Tsz-Nephilimus Sapien would be much different than in modern Homo sapiens.

The human body is complex in terms of construction and identification of parts, but is simple in examination of where everything is located. The human body is like a road map that can be navigated by seeing where all the parts are connected, and where everything made within the body goes and functions. Looking at the secretion of hormones from the pituitary gland throughout the body tells where growth hormone connects and makes the organs, bones, and limbs grow. Think of the human body like an old/new map. An old map would show certain buildings, roads, and landmarks that over time would possibly be replaced or built over and would not appear on a new map. Looking at ancient DNA of humans reveals genetic factors, loci variants, and Mendelian traits affected by environment.

When observed, newer humans of hundreds, thousands, and millions of years advanced. This would then make the next generation (children) from a previous generation (parents) have very different bodies for different reasons. Genetic factors would be different, removed, enhanced, or mutated because of environmental factors, physiology differences, who the parents are, and other factors for the change can occur in the gene pool.

The human body adapts to survive. More specifically, with changing times and multiple needs to survive by adaption factors causes genes, loci, small cells, and hormones to change to fit the circumstances to survive. Looking from a non-procreation angle, humans get new cells all the time. Humans get new cells in their bodies every seven years throughout their lives. This means that for every seven years that passes in one's life, everything is made brand new, renewed, and refreshed. A lot can happen to a person in seven years.

Dealing with human genetics and traits that result in height can be defined from biological continuum and derived traits. Biological continuum is the passing on of traits by means of genetics when expressions of a phenomenon continuously grade into one another so that there are no discrete categories that then exist on a continuum. Derived traits refer to characteristics that are modified from the ancestral condition and thus diagnostic of particular evolutionary lineages. Both of these coincide with what is known as plasticity.

Plasticity, also called phenotypic plasticity, refers to the ability to be shaped or formed, and can change its phenotype in response to changes in the environment. Phenotypes are triggered on the cellular level by the genotypes (cellular genetic makeup markers in cells) that determine specific characteristics that the outside physical body will portray. This means that what effects the genes will ultimately effect everything else outside and inside of the body.

Every giant that is mentioned in the Bible carries the factor of enormous height. They carry the height trait of all the pre-flood giants in their genetic make-up. Their biological continuum is taken directly from the original Tsz-Nephilimus Sapiens. The derived traits of height of each giant mentioned in the books of the Bible are linked to the last purest ancestral lineages of Tsz-Nephilimus Sapien.

Biblical giants were of an extraordinary height. Each giant of the Bible has belonged to a particular people tribe, family, or been identified as a single individual. The giants of the land of Canaan were made up of multiple tribes and ethnicities. This different ethnicity factor would most likely play a role in heights and abilities of the giants. The tribes we know of that were tribes of giants or had giants in them were the Amorites, Emim, Zuziz, Zazummim, Rephaim, Anakim, Egyptians, and Philistines (there possibly were others but these are the ones identified by name). The Egyptians and the Philistines did not have full but rather mixed people of giants and normal humans. The same can be said of the Amorites.

The mixing of different people has often occurred in societies. The idea of giant humans and normal humans living together is quite possible. The mixing of people among the Egyptians, Philistines, and Amorites leads to one particular question. How many giant men and women lived among normal sized humans?

According to Amos 2:9-10, the Amorites were as tall as the cedars and strong as oak trees. In Deuteronomy 3:11, King Og of Bashan stood between 13 and 18 feet tall. This measurement is taken from the size of Og's iron bed stand, which actually is in reference to his coffin instead of an actual bed. In 1 Samuel 17:4-7, Goliath was between 9 to 13 feet in size. These two giants heights vary based on the length of cubit used for measurement. 1 Chronicles 11:23 lists an Egyptian of at least 7 to 9 feet in length. The height factor for these men is substantial. People will always consider it a stretch of belief to admit that men and women were over ten feet tall. The reality though is that this level of height is possible.

Early environmental and atmospheric conditions of earth made it biologically possible for the various human species to be much larger. Ancient earth was once thriving with stronger oxygen levels, cycles of interactions within the biosphere, and biological contribution that fed into the life cycles of earth by living creatures play a part in the ancient beginnings of mega size in plants, animals, and mankind.

Archaic primate orders of humans and apes are believed to be large in size. Homo Heidelbergenesis is thought to have reached heights of up to seven feet. Their height is not brought on by conditions of gigantism or acromegaly (enlarged body parts and organs). Usually one ore two individuals contract gigantism or acromegaly, but to have multiple groupings of people reaching seven feet in length is not a disease or abnormality that multiple people contract. If one generation after another reached a height of seven feet, then this would be an inherited or hereditary trait. Gigantism and acromegaly is not a hereditary condition. These humans had a natural size that was common within the species. Aside from height, we can see a difference in width and height in the physical characteristics of Tsz-Nephilimus Sapien.

CHAPTER 8: WIDTH & STRENGTH

Homo Neanderthalensis, also called the Neanderthal, had 30% more mass than Homo Sapiens. This example from Neanderthals is seen in other extinct human species. As mentioned earlier, an average Neanderthal woman is said to be able to beat a professional arm wrestling champion because her strength and joints contain more strength and flexibility. This kind of strength is inherited in the Neanderthal's genes from one generation to another.

I spend a great deal of time in the gym on average. One thing I notice when I am there is the massive physiques that the male and female members possess. Training the body requires great patience, determination, and study. The human body was designed to adapt to any change that it encounters. This is a common trait among all life, adapt to survive.

Ecclesiastes 1:7 states, "*All streams run to the sea, but the sea is not full; to the place where the streams flow, there they flow again* (ESV)." A person goes to the gym to build muscle, lose weight, gain strength, or get healthy in other areas. The goal of anyone of these reasons is the body gets trained inside and out in order to adapt to all its changes so it can reach the desired outcome. While I train in multiple areas to stay fit and healthy, my primary focus group is bodybuilding and powerlifting.

Bodybuilding is defined as the use of progressive resistance exercise to control and develop one's musculature. Powerlifting is defined as a strength-based competition and strength based set of exercises that is performed at a maximal weight in lifts called the squat, bench press, and deadlift. Both styles of training focus on developing the body's muscles, bones, ligaments, and tendons for peak performance. They also focus, though at varied levels respectively, at building strength.

The physical bodies of every member of a gym vary based on two areas. These are the actual training of the body, and physiology. Physiology is the scientific study of the normal functions of organs, organ systems, cells, and biomolecules and other features in living systems. This sub-discipline of biology is important to understand when entering into any activity involving the human body. What affects the inner workings of the body affects the outer workings. Training includes weight training, nutrition, cardio, calisthenics, rest, diet, supplements, vitamins, and other factors for overall effective and proper training. The physiological depends on the body type of each person training.

Body type, also constitution type, is the different classification systems or typology systems used to classify empirical or theoretical body shapes of an individual. Male and female body types differentiate on several levels. However, both fall under the same body type classifications. The three body types are ectomorph, mesomorph, and endomorph.

Ectomorph bodies have small frame and bone structure, thinned out upper and lower body proportions, fast metabolism, and difficult muscle and weight gaining setbacks. Mesomorphs are athletic, hard bodied, well-defined muscles, rectangular physique, strong, and gain muscle and fat easily. Endomorphs have soft, rounded physiques, gain muscle and fat easily, have short and stocky stature, slow metabolism, hard to lose fat, and muscles that are often not well defined. These body types apply to all modern humans.

While all humans of the modern age share these body type varieties; many other physiological traits have disappeared with the passage of time. Earlier traits would no doubt disappear in later generations, as the need for them to survive would no longer be needed. A physical trait that is no longer needed should be eliminated from the body, as it holds no value for function in every day life.

Matthew 7:17-19 states, *"So every healthy tree bears good fruit, but the diseased tree bears bad fruit. A healthy tree cannot bear bad fruit, nor can a diseased tree bear good fruit. Every tree that does not bear good fruit should be cut down and thrown into the fire* (ESV)."

What isn't needed in the body is removed if it serves no purpose.

At the gym, the members strive for physical perfection. No one can ever truly be perfect. That doesn't mean that we shouldn't attempt to gain perfection. Pushing hard to become better than what I was before I entered the gym meant that I had accomplished something with my time there. To reach my goals and post goals mean I will always have to work harder to get them. For Tsz-Nephilimus Sapien however, the feats I strive for would be child's play.

The human body contains what is known as growth differentiation factors. Growth differentiation factor, or GDF, is a subfamily of proteins from the transforming growth factor beta family that mainly function in physical and physiological development. GDF proteins are classed by number identifications. These proteins are totaled at eleven and identified as GDF-1, GDF-2, GDF-3, GDF-5, GDF-6, GDF-7, GDF-8, GDF-9, GDF-10, GDF-11, and GDF-15. Each of the proteins listed are a part of the TGF superfamily that are made up of greater and lesser proteins. Of all the GDF proteins, GDF 8 and GDF 11 are of main interest.

GDF-8 and GDF-11 play big roles in keeping the body well balanced. These proteins are known as inhibitor proteins. Inhibitor comes from the word inhibit meaning to restrain or limit. Beginning with GDF-8, we see the holy grail of muscle growth in this protein. Identified by it's scientific name, Myostatin, GDF-8 was first discovered in 1997 by geneticists Se-Jin Lee and Alexandra Mcpherron.

These two geneticists created a strain of highly muscular

mice dubbed "mighty mice" after the massive amount of muscle the mice acquired. The mice contained twice the muscle amount of normal mice. This wonder of science was the result of suppressing the myostatin already suppressing the muscles of the mice. By suppressing the suppressant protein in the mice, their muscles began to grow at an exponential rate. The impressive muscular physique of the mice soon followed. While the results of the mighty mice were the result of artificial means by suppressing the GDF-8 protein, there have been natural occurring instances found in multiple animal species and human beings.

What is so significant about inhibitor proteins? In truth, nothing is significant about inhibitor proteins when they are active. It's when they are suppressed that makes them important. When GDF-8 is turned off becoming – GDF-8, (the minus sign representing negative) then what is called the Activin Receptor Type II B or ActRIIB turns muscle growth from off to on. With ActRIIB on, then bones grow stronger, muscles grow, strength increases, and fat burns faster. Suppression of GDF-8 or myostatin can be done naturally or artificially.

To suppress myostatin by artificial means is done by introducing a decoy version of ActRIIB for myostatin to latch itself on to keep it inactive. The natural way consists of possessing a mutated myostatin to promote muscle mass, or lacking the gene entirely for GDF-8 production. Natural myostatin deficiencies occur in humans, cattle, and K-9 species such as Whippets. The cattle species known as Belgian Blue Cattle often grow with tremendous muscles and strength. Their natural developed muscles are a hereditary trait and not a random fluke of nature. Possessing a 40%

increase in natural muscle mass, Belgian Blue Cattle, both male and female, are highly valued for their high yield protein containing meat (Piedmontese meat).

While able to produce naturally, Belgian Blue Cattle have some birthing difficulties due to the large, bulky, and heavy offspring they produce. These cattle are produced through selective breeding due to the delicate birthing process, and a desire to produce only the purest of negative myostatin bloodlines. This selective breeding has been going on for hundreds of years among breeders, ranchers, and farmers.

The significance of mentioning Belgian Blue Cattle has to do with the hereditary genetic traits that have been passed down for those hundreds of years of breeding. Though done through selective breeding, the Belgian Blue Cattle produce natural genetically attributed offspring that each lineage possesses to continue producing viable offspring of the same pure bloodlines. Humans today are rarely born with suppressed or mutated myostatin in their bodies. Those that do possess amazing physiques and incredible strength.

Certain documentaries, news reports, and articles teach us about children born with incredible physiques, physiologies, and strengths not ordinarily seen in children between the ages of three to eight. These children have been either diagnosed or speculated on having mutated or suppressed myostatin. Imagine what these children's strength factors and physiques will be when they reach maturity. Based on the benefits of a natural occurring physiological trait that increases strength, mass, size, and a herculean physique; these children could be labeled as superhuman. While these human specimens in the modern age are rare, it could be very possible many ancient human species possessed these negative myostatin physiques and physiologies.

The protein GDF-11 or neumystatin plays a part in nerve tissue growth, and in the process of natural aging. GDF-11, also called Bone Morphogenetic Protein 11 or BMP-11, is an inhibitor of nerve tissue growth as a result of being a myostatin-homologus protein. GDF-11 and GDF-8 have similar mechanisms to control tissue size in muscular and neural development. GDF-11 has been tested and described as an anti-aging factor.

GDF-11 can have an effect on the central nervous system. It helps improve cerebral vasculature (movement of blood through blood vessels supplying the brain), and enhances neurogenesis (the birth of neurons). With increased blood circulation comes more oxygen flow to extremities, the heart, arteries, and muscles. This increase in blood flow and circulation can help cell growth, better function of organs, healthier skin, and gives the heart more relaxation and a lower heart rate. Blood circulation can also help reduce diabetes and increase brain function. The anti-aging effects are numerous. The most significant effect is the reverse age-related cardiac (heart) hyperthrophy (growth or increase) that keeps the heart at a healthy size.

The heart increases either by exercise, abnormal circumstances, or other ways that require or force the heart to grow to keep up with bodily changes. Cardiac or Ventricular Hypertrophy can be a benefit to a person if it happens during normal responses that the heart goes through during such times as exercise or pregnancy. Unhealthy heart growth happens because of stress, disease, injuries that happen to the heart, heart failure, and other negative factors. These kinds of negative heart increase can make what is called pathological hypertrophy occur.

Pathological hypertrophy can lead to heart muscle mass increase, but won't increase heart pumping ability that can lead to myocardial scarring (collagen) that can disrupt the electrical conduction system of the heart (the rhythm of the heartbeat), and also irritate ventricular myocytes (the muscle cells in the heart muscles) and depolarize them. With the human body being comprised of thirty percent muscle makes it imperative to keep the heart muscles properly sized and regulated for proper growth, blood flow, and respiratory functions.

The enlargement of the heart can occur from diseases such as gigantism. An abnormality such as gigantism can cause heart problems due to the constant growth effects. Humans not affected by the abnormalities of disease or abnormal circumstances of growth could live longer, have more energy, endurance, rejuvenation, and be able to heal much faster. All this because of suppressed GDF-11.

I remember watching the movie Troy. In the first scene, Brad Pitt's character Achilles does battle with a giant soldier named Boagrius. An actor named Nathan Jones played the character of Boagrius. Boagrius was a seven foot, muscle bound soldier who was the greatest warrior of his people (the Thessalonians). In the scene, Achilles kills Boagrius to prove he is the greatest hero and warrior of the Greeks.

What I found interesting about Boagrius was his size, strength, physique, and power. Though a brief cameo,

Boagrius had an amazing spear throw and attack speed when he was running at Achilles (before getting skewered in the left trapezia by Achilles and dying instantly). The actor, who played Boagrius, Nathan Jones, is an impressive individual. Born in Australia, Jones stood at seven feet tall and weighed three hundred and fifty pounds. He was a world champion power lifter, World's Strongest Man competition champion, professional wrestling champion, and a mixed martial artist. For a man standing seven feet tall, Nathan Jones is incredibly strong, flexible, fast, and athletic. Seeing a man like this in real life and playing an ancient Greek warrior made me picture just what ancient giants and other human species could have resembled.

We get to see how strong some of these mighty men of the Bible were in three scriptures. The first to have detailed descriptions of his strength and stature would be the Philistine Goliath. In 1 Samuel 17:4-7 we read, *"And there went out a champion out of the camp of the Philistines named Goliath, of Gath, whose height was six cubits and a span. And he had a helmet of brass upon his head, and he was armed with a coat of mail; and the weight of the coat was five thousand shekels of brass. And he had greaves of brass upon his legs, and a target of brass between his shoulders. And the staff of his spear was like a weaver's beam; and his spear's head weighed six hundred shekels of iron: and one bearing a shield went before him (KJV)."* Let's convert these shekel weights into pounds.

To compare briefly, an average American soldier or marine carries about 60 pounds of gear out in the field with the occasional doubling of the weight due to patrols or other assignments requiring the extra load. This would come to about 120 pounds (give or take) total. Special forces can often carry about 90 pounds of gear without occasional addition unlike regular soldiers.

As seen in the scripture, Goliath had a vast amount of armor and gear each with its own individual weight. The weight of Goliath's coat of mail or chain armor would have weighed between 125 to 157 pounds. It has been estimated that the actual weight of Goliath's chain armor was at least 130 pounds based upon the thickness of the brass. Good chain armor had to be thick enough to withstand a dart, arrow, spear, or sword thrust.

The Philistines were famous for being among the first warriors to use straight blades for stabbing as opposed to more curved designed weapons that were used for slashing opponents. It would be natural to assume they would build armor that could withstand both enemy weaponry, as well as their own since there were other people using straight bladed weaponry. Needing metal that would repel armor piercing weapons of iron, brass would be an ideal metal to use in construction of armor. Brass is a soft metal, but sturdy and strong enough to withstand iron weapons.

The brass helmet, leg greaves, and target brass from his shoulders weight must have also been considerable. Though from a different time period, the best guess for the weight of Goliath's helmet could be similar to the Spartan Hoplite helmet of the 4th and 5th centuries called a *pilos*. Spartan helmets were mainly made of bronze, though with small traces of tin, lead, and iron added. A *pilos* helmet combined with Spartan leg greaves often added 20 to 30 pounds to the Spartan warrior on top of the weight the rest of their bronze armor and shield gave them.

Spartans were well trained and well built warriors. To carry around a lot of weight packed on by their armor would be child's play to them. It would not be a far stretch to assume Goliath's helmet and leg greaves (though made of brass would probably have more weight due to his size and width) would be close to 30 pounds of brass in total weight assuming that was the maximum (the weight could have been possibly closer to 40 pounds). His shoulder guards could have weighed about 15 to 20 pounds. In the gym, I can wear and move well in a 20 pound weighted vest that covers my shoulders and chest. The weight vest I wear fits my 6'3 frame. Goliath, being nine to 12 feet tall would at least be able to carry 20 pounds on his shoulders. Combining these weights in total, Goliath would be wearing about 207 or more pounds in armor.

Goliath's spearhead was made of iron weighing six hundred shekels. 600 shekels of iron weight equal 15 pounds. A weaver's beam, which is fabric spun together for use in fabric making, could refer to the thickness of the spears handle, and the type of spear Goliath used. The weaver's beam, also called the string spear or veritum (from the Latin word veritus meaning revered or feared) was an innovative piece of wartime hardware from the Bronze Age. With a yard range of 8, 16, 24, 36, or 70 yards when thrown, the weaver's beam could be used on foot or mounted chariot. This spear was believed to have been a major asset in securing victories for the Assyrian and Hittite armies. Having a 15 pound iron spearhead and thrown by a man of Goliath's height and strength could spell big trouble for anybody on the receiving end of the weaver's beam. This would bring the total amount of armor and weapons weight Goliath was carrying close to

221 pounds.

Goliath's shield and sword must have also been of a good sized weight for effective offensive and defensive capabilities. Goliath's weapons would have to be proportionate to meet the demands of his size. Goliath's shield would be made of brass like the rest of his armor. Using the armaments of the Spartans, their bronze shield weighed up to 24 pounds with a 36-inch height and width, as it was a rounded shield. Since Goliath used an armor bearer to carry his shield, it would be a good estimate that his shield was also 20 pounds or more. Goliath's sword would be made of iron instead of brass. Since the straight sword was used by the Philistines in favor of the curved or sickle sword, Goliath's blade would be a straight blade. A standard sword of iron would be about 4 to 5 pounds. Goliath's would be about 5 to 6 pounds due to the size, the weight of the iron used, and the hilt or handle that the blade was attached. If we were to imagine Goliath using a standard Philistine blade, then he would be wielding a sword that would resemble a knife or dagger due to it being made for a man (or woman) of lesser height and width. A standard sword might not be able to be used by Goliath, as it might not fit properly in his hand. The sword would have to be custom made for him.

Philistine swords were typically made of iron and bronze. Bronze was used for the hilt or handle as it was heavier than iron. This would help give the sword more weight in the hand and arm to aid in the swing or thrust of the blade. Iron was what the blade was forged from because of its lighter weight and harder hitting power as compared to bronze. The typical sword of the Mediterranean was a single edged bladed sword called the sickle sword. It was primarily used for slashing and cutting.

The two most common used sickle swords were the Assyrian Sapara and the Egyptian Khopesh. Both types of blades were cast from a single piece of bronze with no hand or knuckle guard for protection. Philistine culture evolved out of Mycenaean Greek culture. Their weapons and combat tactics reflected the Greek culture. This would explain the technological advances and effectiveness the Philistines brought to the wars they fought (in one battle with Israel they killed over 30,000 soldiers). Goliath's sword is one example of their technological superiority. In pictures and paintings Goliath is often depicted as using a sickle sword. Sickle blades are a limited fighting weapon. Goliath was a spearman in the Philistine army. Spearman were infantry units. They made up the backbone of the ancient world's armies. The Spartans seen in the movie 300 were spearman. They used shield and spear for their Phalanx (a shield and spear defensive and offensive position), and for engaging enemies in other close range attacks.

Philistines came form Mycenaean Greece. Their cultural similarities are made evident in architecture, pottery, politics, and military. Their use of Goliath in single combat against an opposing armies greatest warrior is based on Homeric combat strategies found throughout Mycenaean culture (and in the books *the Iliad* and *the Odyssey* by Homer). From Mycenae, we get a piece of pottery called the Warrior Vase. The pot is dated to be from the 13th Century BCE. The imagery on the pot depicts armored soldiers. These soldiers are the most artistic rendering of what Goliath might have looked like in his armor.

Goliath's armor and weaponry were unique in the Middle East. After King David killed Goliath with his own sword, he took his armor and weapons and separated them. After David went on the run as an outlaw from King Saul for fear David would depose Saul, David took Goliath's sword as his own. David had no weapon of his own when he went on the run from King Saul. A priest named Ahimelech gave aid to David when he came to him. Ahimelech gave David the sword of Goliath so he would not be without a weapon.

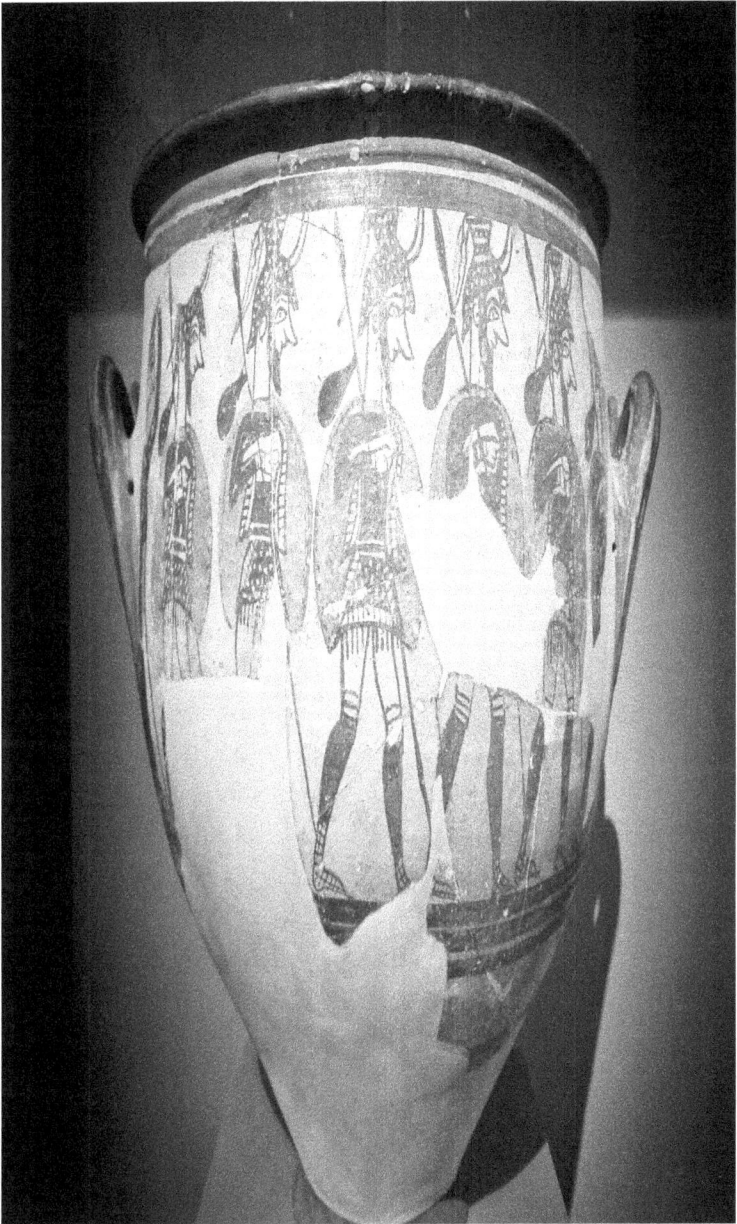

Warrior Vase Courtesy of Sharon Mollerus

1 Samuel 21:9 says, *"And the priest said, the sword of Goliath, whom thou slewest in the valley of Elah, behold it is here thou wilt take that, take it: for there is no other save that here. And David said, there is none like that; give it to me* (KJV)." Notice David uses the words 'there is none like that.' Goliath's sword was not like any other weapon. Israel and other Middle East weapons were not top of the line. Any weapons that were high grade were the result of countries or empires with a lot of money to spend on good materials and craftsmen from their own people, or from reliable traders that had the means to procure such weapons or materials to forge by their own people.

Those who could not afford good metal ore built their weapons from copper or lesser materials that were not as strong as bronze or iron. With the introduction of the bronze and Iron Age came the chance for each tribe, nation, or empire to get better at the art of making weapons. However, many people were not rich, skilled in better weapons crafting, and had a distance to go before they could get good enough to fight with reliable weapons against the more advanced civilizations. In short, no two Bronze Age and Iron Age civilizations that could make weapons were alike.

Goliath's sword was unique among the Israelites because it most likely was Greek in its design. Technologically, Goliath's blade was made of iron with the handle made of bronze. For his height, between nine to twelve inches tall, Goliath would have to have a sword of exceptional length. This length would not be a ridiculous size, but a reasonably exceptional size and weight to suit his needs. The typical length of an Aegean and Mediterranean sword was about 26 to 31 inches in length, with a weight of about 2.5 to 4.5

pounds. This made swords small but effective to wield, and capable of being carried on the hip, back, or occasionally on or within a shield. Swords like this were long enough to be effective on foot, horseback, or chariot, yet small enough and light to avoid more difficulty from complicated moves or postures normally attributed with longer weapons. Goliath's sword would be at best around 40 inches in length with a weight of five to six pounds. Goliath, while a giant, would only be enough feet taller to require a weapon slightly longer than one that could be wielded by someone about six feet tall. His blade would fit his size, but would appear to be a standard military issue sword. This would be because the blacksmiths and metallurgists who made the Philistines weapons would only need to vary slightly from their usual forges and castings to accommodate a larger soldier such as Goliath. The extra foot and weight of Goliath's sword design could be applied to other giants of the Philistine army.

There is one sword in today's world that could be from the time of the Philistine giants. Whether it is or is not of the era of King David isn't fully known, but what is known is it originates from the Jewish people. In Istanbul, Turkey, there is a sword on display at the Topkapi Museum called the Al-Battar sword. Al-Battar means 'the one who cuts through.' The sword is 39.76 inches long, making it 3 feet and 3.76 inches in length. The sword belonged to a Jewish tribe named the Banu Qaynaqa. They lived in 7th century Medina as possible descendants of Joseph's son Manasseh. The Islamic Prophet Mohammed confiscated the sword after expelling them from Medina for political reasons. The sword became part of a collection of swords Mohammed owned. Later, it made its way to Turkey where it remains on display for all to see at the museum. The blade is a straight, double-edged sword that fits the description of what Goliath's and the other giant's swords could have looked like.

Other giants of the Philistines used unique armor and weaponry. Goliath had four brothers who served in the Philistine army. We read about them in 2 Samuel 21:16-22. Ishbi Benob, the first brother mentioned, carried a spear with a spearhead that weighed about eleven pounds. He also carried a new sword. Though the details of the weapon are unknown, it is likely Ishbi Benob had a sword of equal size to the one Goliath used. He is famous for being the man that almost killed David when David was too exhausted to continue fighting during a battle with the Philistines.

Another brother, whose name is unknown, carried a spear whose shaft was as big as a weavers beam. 1 Chronicles 11:23 has an Egyptian giant who wielded a spear like a weaver's beam. It could be assumed that Goliath's other brothers carried specialized weaponry of unique size and weight. It would be best to surmise that all these men were spearmen, the backbone of an ancient army infantry unit.

One interesting question to be asked is why would anyone make a spearhead that weighed eleven to fifteen pounds? One answer is that such a heavy tipped spear would be very effective when thrown. When throwing a spear, there are three things needed for a good throw. One is a balancing point on the handle to make the spear even and level. Ancient spears would at times have what is called pommels on the bottom of the spear to act as a counter balance to the spearhead, while others had shafts that were equal to the weight of the spearhead to avoid the need for a pommel. The second is a spear must be thrown in an arc. An arc is a curved line or differentiable curved line that looks like a half circle. The arc throw leads to the third and final piece of the perfect throw, top heavy. The spear has to be thrown in an arc curve to keep the spearhead top heavy. This keeps all the weight in the spearhead to ensure that it sticks when it lands. It also helps for the spear to go through an opponent to kill them. For men of Goliath's height and strength to be considered great spear throwers would be an understatement.

Like swords, the Philistines would use spears of Greek design. The description of the weaver's beam spear from earlier fits the description of the spears used in the late Bronze and Iron Age weapons of the Middle East by Hittites, Assyrians, and the Philistine people. Being late-bronze to early Iron Age, the spears would be both wood and iron. The term weaver's beam that is used to describe many of the giant's spears is not a length of measurement, but the thickness of the wood handle or shaft. An actual weaver's beam varies in length depending on what is being made.

Greeks of the 1600 to 100 BC era used long spears. The length of a Greek long spear is eight to nine feet long. This was the standard for both spearman and chariot warriors. The eight foot long spear could be wielded by most soldiers, as it was a balanced weapon. A spear past eight feet was not impossible to use, but very difficult to wield, as it was unbalanced and clumsy. Spears of eight feet were equal in length, and could be balanced between the spearhead and the arm holding it.

Spartan warriors carried eight-foot long spears that weighed 5.5 pounds. A mid-range weapon, the spearhead carried on a Spartan spear carried slightly more weight, but was evened out by the arm strength of the Spartan. Spartans carried a bronze shield that weighed 24 pounds. It's easy to surmise the Spartans had the arm strength to balance their odd weight spears for maximum thrust and occasional throws.

The spears of the giants would be odd length weapons. The odd length would make a spearhead of eleven to fifteen pounds suitable for an uneven handle that is or exceeds nine feet. This would help them to be effective spearman in a mechanized unit, have an effective mid-range weapon to stab, slash, or throw at an enemy, and use for one-on-one combat when the occasion for single combat was necessary. The details of the armor and weaponry show the strength of the giants. Though their complete physical strength factors are not fully known, we do witness a degree of it from these details. From their strengths come a considerable weight advantage compared to average humans.

CHAPTER NINE: WEIGHT

The tallest man of the modern century was named Robert Wadlow. He reached a height of eight feet and eleven inches. He weighed a total of 439 pounds. Wadlow suffered from gigantism and hyperplasia (increased organ tissue and enlarged organs). He passed away at the age of 22 in 1940. A giant from our present day is Jorge Gonzales from Argentina. Standing seven feet and seven inches tall, Jorge weighed about 460 pounds. He suffered from Gigantism, and passed away in 2010 at the age of 44. He was a basketball player and professional wrestler. He could run well, had good flexibility in his legs and arms, and was strong enough to lift men weighing 300 to 400 pounds. Other giants in pro wrestling that were past seven feet tall include Andre the giant from France (7'4), Giant Silva from Brazil (7'2), Daliph Singh Rana from India (7'1), and Paul White from America (7').

Many of these men weighed over 300, 400, and 500 pounds. While some suffered from gigantism and acromegaly, they were flexible, strong, could move at adequate to good speeds, and carried their weight well for men of proportional size. Many of them also had and have incredible physiques.

Daliph Singh Rana was a two-time Mr. India in bodybuilding, and competed in powerlifting before entering professional wrestling. It is rumored that he lifted boulders in India when he worked a job (legitimately) in a rock quarry. Daliph trains, lifts weights, and maintains a good diet, but has a natural physical strength that appeared before he began his athletic career. Professional wrestling is sports entertainment, but it has real athletes with natural talent. Many things can and are said about the athletes in professional wrestling, but the giant men and women of the sport do have one thing that is known. They have strength, size, and weight that is a result of the genetics from their natural birth.

These wrestlers, while impressive, often have genetic diseases that are a blessing and a curse. Modern medicine and surgical procedures have helped significantly fight the genetic defects such as gigantism, hyperplasia, and acromegaly. Outside of genetic disease and defects, many people are born both tall and with weight brought on as a result of their size. Weight and height go hand in hand. The scientist Galileo created what he called the Square Cube Law. The definition of the square cube law is as any object grows, its volume grows faster than its surface area. This means that because the area grows proportionally to the square of its size, the volume grows proportionally to the cube of the size. In short, a surface area can increase (for example) by a factor of 100, but its volume will increase by a factor of 1,000.

If isometrically scaled up to considerable amounts, a person's relative strength would be severely reduced. This is a result of the cross sections of the muscles increasing by the square of the scaling factor. Its mass, however, would increase by the cube of the scaling factor. Cardiovascular and respiratory functions would be affected by this result. Galileo's view, however, is not quite accurate. His work is, at best, an approximation for moderate human and animal sizes. It can explain much, but lacks in certain areas that can be explained with other sciences.

The study of allometry expands the horizons of the square cube law. Allometry is the study of the relationship of body size to shape, anatomy, physiology, and behavior. Galileo is correct to a point in his claim that a human can lift only an amount equal to his own weight because of relative muscular strength. However, no two people are the same equally in strength and physique. Square cube law and allometry focus on physiological cross-sectional areas of muscle physiology. PSCA, or physiological cross-sectional area, is the cross-sectional area of a muscle perpendicular to its fibers. This is usually at its largest point.

Galileo made an approximation of how big and strong people can become. Mass and volume are not limited to what we inherit from birth. The body doesn't get weaker from more weight or volume in the body mass (unless you are in really bad shape or sick). The body doesn't always get stronger with more muscle mass. A bodybuilder can look like a Greek god, and yet be as strong as an average man. A power lifter can weigh 500 pounds, but his bones and physical frame can support the weight and be able to lift or push over 1,000 pounds. Muscle fibers, proteins, sarcoplasms (the fluid in muscle cells that correlate less or more strength depending on how much is in the muscles), and water weight can all play variables in strength, weight, physique, flexibility, and movement (walking and running). People who are born with good genetics can defy the square cube law easily.

Each cross section of muscle is composed of fast and slow twitch fibers that help in making the body go fast, have bursts of energy for speed and strength so we don't burn out fast from exhaustion. The fibers that build up strength are fast twitch fibers. A ton of fast-twitch fibers will make a man or woman much stronger. Size doesn't matter when the body is primed to be a physical specimen through natural and artificial means. Modern humans change their bodies everyday through weight training, cardio, supplements, and medical procedures.

Isaiah 43:18-19 says, "*Remember ye not the former things, neither consider the things of old. Behold, I will do a new thing; now it shall spring forth; shall ye not know it? I will even make a way in the wilderness, and rivers in the desert* (KJV)." Mankind today builds cities in the desert, makes islands in the oceans, and runs rivers in desolate places. The dead matter of the earth can be used to extract material to make fuel (fossil fuels), create life, and expand on what already lives to be bigger, better, and healthier. This is the reality of man who is like God. Man can't do everything God can, but they can come close.

Just like with artificial means, life can change naturally. If a person is born with high-twitch muscle fibers, then they can grow over time to develop hand in hand with neuromuscular coordination (the balancing of everything in the body based on height, width, and weight). In young people, all strength and power factors can improve bone density, lean muscle mass, neuromuscular coordination, maintain contractility of muscle fibers, and create better hormonal response. Taking into account the benefits of suppressed GDF-8 and GDF-11 proteins, the body would be able to develop the natural strength, muscle mass, blood, and oxygen flow to aide in growth to large size, maintain strong bone density (density is the over all factor that determines the strength of bones), and carry on an exceeding amount of weight that would normally crush bones, cartilage, and limit mobility.

If the bones and cartilage can maintain the stress on what is called the articular-area of limb-bone cartilage, then men and women of great height and weight can move like average humans with no problems. Natural bodies change over time for multiple reasons. Depending on when the person was born, where they were born, and what conditions surround their birth such as parentage and genes, a body could have unnatural or uncommon attributes and traits. Mutations, abnormalities, and diseases can occur as a result of unique bloodlines and hybrid human species.

CHAPTER 10: ANOMALIES & MUTATIONS

In the last chapter we covered what the body or bodies of Tsz- Nephilimus Sapien and their descendants would have in terms of physical and physiological traits. However, one real question remains. How did they get their height? One other question that would follow is what are the side effects of being born a giant? Are there any mutations that follow?

Random variables have always played a part in the changes of life. Nature, geology, space, and even time have all been affected by variables that occurred during random and purposeful events. One group of organisms that were affected by life changes is known as Megafauna. Megafauna is defined as large animals. Megafauna classification of size includes weights that exceed 100 to 220 pounds. Humans are included in megafauna classification. This type of size does not deal predominately with extremely large animals, but can also deal with small yet heavy animals. However, megafauna predominately is identified with mammals, reptiles, birds and other species that were usually past 10 feet in height and length. Megafauna can be identified by the trophic levels or food web positions they occupy in terms of their predatory status as herbivores, carnivores, and omnivores. This means that each animal can be affected by similar ecological conditions that affect animals in or around a particular area of various climate and environmental conditions. These conditions can determine how an animal survives, adapts, migrates, or becomes extinct based on the conditions of an area affecting a particular species or multiple species.

Biology is affected by the conditions of an environment or ecological differentiation. Megafauna are considered to be a result of an ecological niche that, under certain environmental conditions, could grow at a greater rate of length and size in a shorter time span. This rate of increased size could eventually be overtaken by normalized size factors in later generations of animal and human species that would have a greater rate of body mass decrease as opposed to increase. This is a result of several major changes in the time epochs and events of earth's history.

Daniel 2:43 states, "*And whereas thou sawest iron mixed with miry clay, they shall mingle themselves with the seeds of men: but they shall not cleave one to another, even as iron is not mixed with clay* (KJV)." This scripture refers to the mixing of bloods of different races. It should be noted that humanity is called a race, but the term for the human race is for humanity as a whole. There is no difference between people who are different colors or look different than someone else. Race is just a political term that is only acceptable on occasion to classify different species with several different variations within that species.

The scripture in Daniel 2:43 tells us a few realities about making hybrid species. Using the example of mixing clay and iron, any two materials have to be either chemically bonded or able to mix properly for a new element to be produced. This can be seen with copper and tin being mixed together (though not chemically bonded) to make bronze. Clay and iron are elements that don't mix together. Anything mixed together may or may not bond well, but something can and does usually come from the mixing of different elements. Whether it's a good or bad end result is the question to ask.

Most megafauna died out at certain points in history. Australia's megafuana became extinct 45,000 years ago. North American megafauna became extinct 16,000 years ago. These animals lived during the late Cenozoic Era just after the extinction of the dinosaurs. Megafauna thrived predominately during the Pleistocene Era of the last ice age, which ended around 14,500 years ago. This puts the North American megafuana just 2,000 years behind the end of the last part of the ice age. Megafauna included animals such as the Titanoboa (the largest known snake ever to exist), the Wooly Mammoth, and the Megaterium or Ground Sloth. The last remaining of any of the extinct genus of megafauna ultimately died out 10,000 years ago.

Why did megafauna go extinct? There are several theories thrown around on the subject. The most likely I believe are isolated and conjoining circumstances. Those circumstances would be the appearance of man, disease, and environmental and ecological changes. Using Daniel 2:43 as the guiding light reveals what happens when new non-living and living compounds are produced. Using Homo-Sapiens and Tsz-Nephilimus Sapiens as examples; when new species are made of two different kinds of genetics, then comes with it new blood types and health factors.

Every human species produces two types of nucleic acids, the DNA or deoxyribonucleic acid, and RNA or ribonucleic acid. Both work for the biological components in the biology of mankind. However, RNA can go one step further as it can be used to encode the genetic information of viruses. A virus with an RNA strand is called an RNA virus. This kind of virus has several classes and strands that infect pretty much everything and everyone.

The best surmised answer would be that original viruses originated from within a host species of man and/or animal that over time adapted to changes in its environment. Viruses evolved to more deadly forms, mutated into new viruses, or developed into cross species strains that could infect man and animal alike with little to no difference in symptoms and contagion factors. This would lead to the birth of new kinds of diseases as many viruses turn into common, chronic, epidemic, pandemic, cancer, or cancer types of diseases. Plants can create viruses that infect humans. Many plant viruses are RNA viruses.

The basis of any viral beginning is mutation. Mutation is the permanent alteration of the nucleotide sequencing of the genome of an organism, a virus, or the extra chromosomal DNA and other genetic elements. It results from damage to

DNA that doesn't get repaired, errors made in the process of replication, and from insertion or deletion of segments of DNA by mobile genetic elements. There was another episode of Batman, the Animated Series, that I enjoyed as a child that had a good example of mutation. In the episode an athlete named Anthony Romulus finds a chemical biologist to make him anabolic steroids that won't be detectable during drug inspections. The scientist goes one step further and creates a steroid derivative combining steroid and Timber Wolf estrogen, which heightened Romulus' human body and attributes to their utmost potential and was totally undetectable to drug tests.

When the human body has extra doses of estrogen administered, then the body is tricked into producing large amounts of testosterone to counter the estrogen levels. Testosterone can also be made from the administered estrogen itself. Romulus did get stronger, faster, and had far greater energy. However, his DNA mutated to create a case of Lycanthropy. This is more commonly known as Werewolfism. He went through an early stage, followed by an advanced stage artificially induced by the scientist who gave Romulus the disease. The reason for the mentioning of this story is to give example of the changes brought on by DNA mutation. While, of course, people won't turn into animals, when DNA mutates it will give off unique side effects. One such trait is sometimes seen in giants is a condition known as Polydactyly.

Polydactyly is a congenital, physical anomaly found in humans and animals that involves the growth of extra digits of the hands and feet. This extra growth of body parts is known as supernumerary (multiple) body parts of the interior and exterior organs, limbs, and appendages. Polydactyly is often viewed as both a birth and genetic defect. Most polydactyly cases are associated with normal sized humans and animals. However, there is a connection between polydactyly symptoms and unusual human heights.

Polydactyly is an autosomal (a chromosome that is not a sex chromosome) dominant trait. The allele frequency is very low for polydactyly conditions, which make it a rare condition. It happens in about 1 to 500 births. The three most common cases of polydactyly are found in small communities in India, Africa and African Americans, Australians, Brazilians, and among the Amish in Pennsylvania.

The Old Order Amish have a tendency to intermarry within their community. This can lead to intermarriage between blood related people that will give rise to a high chance of genetic defects, abnormalities, and mental retardation found in their offspring. The genetic drift from marriage to same blood relations leaves very little in the gene pool for new genetic material to form. This causes mutations in the gene pool leading to abnormalities. One interesting point of observation to Amish born with polydactyly are high cases of Ellis-van Creveld Syndrome. This is a type of dwarfism that is genetically inherited. This points out a connection between height and extra digits and other body parts.

We see that giants have been recorded having six (or more as polydactyly is not limited to only six fingers and toes) digits. One of Goliath's brothers had polydactyly on his hands and feet. 2 Samuel 21:20 reads, *"And there was yet another battle in Gath, where a man of great stature, that had on every hand six fingers, and on every foot six toes, four and twenty in number (24); and he also was born to the giant (KJV)."* This mention of a giant with polydactyly adds to the connection between height and extra digits. We see a polydactyly inheritance from people of both short and tall height. The connection between height and polydactyly is made possible via hereditary and environmental factors. The only difference between tall and short is how high and how low they go. The understanding of Goliath's brother being of an excessive height with six functioning fingers is fully acceptable because of the usefulness a sixth finger would be for a soldier.

Polydactyly has three main types of finger positioning. Ulnar or postaxial polydactyly, which places the sixth finger next to the pinky. Radial or preaxial polydactyly, that positions the sixth finger next to the thumb. Then the final type which is central polydactyly, where the sixth finger is next to any of the central fingers more commonly known as the ring, middle, and index fingers. The most common of these types of polydactyly is postaxial polydactyly.

Postaxial polydactyly would also be the most useful if the digit were fully developed. Polydactyly fingers occur as either small nubs that are removed via surgery at a young age since they are not connected to bones or nerves and basically are just excess skin, or fully functioning digits with their own finger bones, joints, and nerves. People born with a functioning sixth finger say they often prefer the sixth finger. Videos of people in Brazil born with six fingers can hold balls with greater dexterity and finger strength, play musical instruments such as guitar and piano very efficiently, and can grab and hold items slightly better than a person with five fingers.

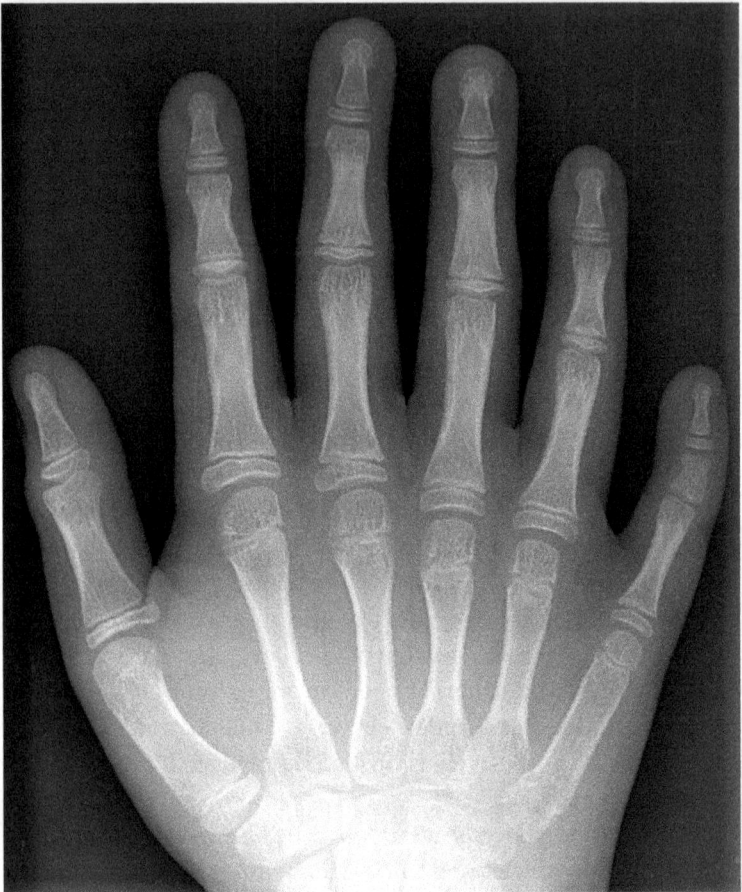

Postaxial Polydactyly right hand x-ray courtesy of Magnus Manske

Depending on Goliath's brother being possibly a spearman like Goliath in the Philistine army, then he'd have a slight edge in carrying his shield and spear. A spear and shield held with a sixth finger would allow slightly better grip strength, balance, and dexterity for throwing, blocking, stabbing, and thrusting motions. Whether he carried a sword like his brothers is not known. Spearmen of the Philistine army, like enlisted men of the U.S. military, carried basic weapons and equipment (spears were standard issue like rifles). However, like modern day special forces, some special weapons and equipment were allowed for particular operations. Goliath and his brothers carried out special assignments (such as individual challenge matches), which required swords, unique equipment, and even armor. Since we don't know the weaponry of the sixth fingered brother, the spear and shield will be best considered his primary weapons and thus are where his sixth finger attributes will be best utilized.

There is not much to be gained from having six toes. Modern people born with six toes face problems of imbalance, finding proper fitting shoes, and carry a risk of having the toes overlapping, grow on top, or over each other. However, if the toes have their own joints and bones then some extra balance could be attained. This would depend on where the toe is, if it was straight like the other five, and if the person with the toe had trained himself or herself to balance themselves instead of living with an imbalance. This has been proven in the sport of boxing as professional boxer Danny Garcia has six toes on his left foot, and says it keeps him from getting off balance in his fights.

Throughout history there have been sightings of giants with polydactyly. In Hawaiian culture there are beliefs that giants with six fingers lived on the islands. The famous hang ten sign is believed to have originated as a sign of a person with six fingers. In Native American culture there are stories of giants with six fingers. The How hand gesture that is used for formal greetings is thought to have originated as a way to tell if a person had six fingers or five. Throughout history are many descriptions of giants or larger men and women with abnormal looking physical characteristics. The world is full of false notions, but some physical descriptions of giants can be true. Aside from polydactyly are beliefs that giants have double rowed teeth. This is a real condition known as Hyperdontia, where supernumerary teeth grow behind other existing teeth. These teeth don't usually make full rows of teeth on the lower or upper jaws, but rather form various shapes and size teeth of one, to a few, or multiple teeth in a disorganized pattern in the mouth. Many extra teeth can form behind or between the central incisors. This is where the most obvious view of extra rows of teeth can be seen from observation. This condition is also affected by hereditary factors, and other genetic reasons such as environment and genetic drift.

Some other physical observations are multiple hair colors spread through regions of the world where those kinds of hair colors such as red or blonde, are not usually seen in the indigenous people of the area. This unique phenomenon of hair color difference is possibly due to the phenotypes pheomelanin (the pigment color genes for red and orange hair) being more dominant as every human has some pheomelanin in his or her hair. Another characteristic is vocal humming or buzzing sounds that the giants made and were very annoying when heard. This trait could be due to more of a type of war cry or diversion tactic similar to what some African tribes used when hunting or going to war. One of the lesser characteristics studied that I am fascinated by is age factor.

If we look at Tsz-Nephilimus Sapien closely, we see their aging factor is surprisingly different from Homo Sapiens. Homo Sapiens used to live up to 900 to 1000 years. This same age factor applies to Tsz-Nephilimus Sapien. If we are to look at all the human species the earth has housed since the time of earliest man, then it is certainly plausible to see man has not always lived a mere hundred and some odd years. From my own studies and research I have yet to find why mankind can't live beyond his average years. The only conclusion I can find is based in Genesis 6:3, "*And the Lord said, My spirit shall not always strive with man, for that he also is flesh: yet his days shall be an hundred and twenty years* (KJV)." Why only 120 years of life? This would have to do with environmental changes happening on the earth. It also has to do with the relationship of God with man, or more specifically the Spirit of God.

John 1:12:13 reads, "*But as many as received Him, to them gave He power to become the sons of God, even to them that believe on His name: which were born, not of blood, nor of the will of the flesh, nor of the will of man, but of God* (KJV)." In technical terms, humans were meant to live forever like the angels of God. Due to the effects of sin, the environmental changes combined with the passage of time, and man's constant, contemporary lifestyle pace of unhealthy habits could leave one to hardly guess why our aging had gone from almost 1,000 years to a mere 120 years lifespan. Tsz-Nephilmus Sapien has a different life span and youth factor. Even when whole species of man or animal die out, there's always a chance some survive before they are totally extinct. When the flood of Noah happened, the chances of survival were slim at best, but not impossible. Throughout the world are accounts of survivors of a great world flood by means of boats similar to the ark of Noah, and by means of ingenious construction tactics by such people as the early ancestors of the Chinese. These stories are controversial, but there is one other possible survivor of the flood that is recorded in Jewish writings. That person is named Og.

Og is possibly from the pure bloodline of Tsz-Nephilimus Sapien. He is mentioned in several books of the Bible. Og was an Amorite king of Bashan. In Deuteronomy 3:11 we read, "*For only Og king of Bashan remained of the remnant of giants;*

behold, his bedstead was a bedstead of iron; is it not in Rabbath of the children of Ammon? Nine cubits was the length thereof, and four cubits the breadth of it, after the cubit of a man (KJV)." He is also mentioned in the books of Numbers and Psalms. Og controlled 60 walled cities in Bashan and several unwalled towns. He is either one of a few or the only other original giant to survive the flood of Noah. This is described in the Hebrew Midrashim and Talmud. According to the Hebrew Midrashim or Midrash, Og survived on a pile of ladders protruding from the ark. Noah discovered him, and after Og basically begged for his life, stayed adrift on the protruding ladders and was fed by Noah.

It is not hard to imagine Noah showing mercy to Og. After surviving the flood, Noah becomes an alcoholic for a time. Being the last survivor of the human race would probably make anyone go into a state of depression with alcohol being seen as a way to forget a devastating flood and end to most life on earth. Perhaps seeing Og struggling to survive made Noah take pity on him. Perhaps he felt that this was a way to justify what was happening to the world around him by saving a life instead of just letting Og slip into a watery grave. Remember, while Noah obeyed God, he was still human. Seeing the world as wicked like God saw it is always possible to understand if it comes from God. But, being human can make a man or woman feel a heavy sense of burden before and after the deed is done. Whatever the reason, Og is considered a survivor of the flood. If true, then this would also make Og be a very advanced age by the time he encountered Moses and Joshua.

The age of Og would be either 900 to 1,000 years old. This age is debatable, as nobody knows exactly how old Og was at the time of his death. Some have estimated him to be close to 896 to 897 years old. My calculations however, have put Og past 910 years (not saying he is 910 years old, but rather he is past the marker of 910 years). When I was working towards my first PHD I did a paper that contained the age of Og. I took into account the possibility of Og being a survivor of the flood. If so, then Og could have been born hundreds of years earlier than estimated. If true, then Og could be older than Methuselah who was 969 years old at the time of his death. Og was a very powerful man. In the Midrashim and Talmud he is described as tossing mountains and boulders at the people of Israel during his wars with them. This is at best a description of Og being strong enough to lift large rocks and hurl them at his enemies because he had the strength and size to be able to lift very heavy weight. Going back to the height of certain giants as examined in the last chapter, Og was very tall. Many have assumed he was about 12 to 15 feet tall.

My estimates based on cubit lengths would be more to about 18 feet in length. The actual length of Og is derived from his iron bed as read in Deuteronomy 3:11. The actual iron bed reference is what describes Og's coffin or sarcophagus. Iron was not used in many beds back in the Bronze Age and Iron Age. The term iron often referred to the color of a black ore that was used for tombs in the land of Canaan and other surrounding areas. Many stone tombs of Bashan and other Middle East countries consisted of basalt, a very hard grey and black stone. There is one other example of a stone sarcophagus that was possibly a giant's tomb that was discovered in the land of Egypt. That tomb belongs to the Egyptian 15th dynasty of rulers known as the Hyskos.

The Hyskos were rulers from Asia who invaded Lower Egypt in 1700 BC. They were not the richest Egyptian empire, but they brought the horse and chariot, Bronze Age weapons, and new techniques of spinning and weaving for making clothes to Egypt. In southern Abydos, Egypt is a series of tombs from the 13th and 15th dynasties. An Egyptian pharaoh named Woseribre Senebkay of the 15th dynasty had one tomb that was a brick structure with a painted limestone block structure. Another Sarcophagus, which was a used tomb, belonged to a king that derived from the 13th dynasty. It weighed over 60 tons and was made of red quartzite. The chamber was transported to Abydos from Gebel Ahmar (present day Cairo), and had housed a previous inhabitant. Who was the occupant of the tomb before it arrived at the resting place of Senebkay is not exactly known. The name Sobekhoteb is believed to be the Pharaoh of the sarcophagus, but which Sobekhoteb (as there are many in the dynasty) is not known for certain due to lack of evidence. However, the size of the inhabitant must have been enormous. The measurement of the length of the tomb is about 12 to 13 feet. Whoever was the previous owner was possibly an ancient giant.

* Unknown Tomb photo courtesy of photographer Josef Wagner, Penn Museum

Og is not the only giant to have been of an advanced age. Goliath himself may have been past 50 by the time he was killed by David. The Jewish Talmud and Midrash give reference to Goliath being present for the battle between Israel and the Philistines in 1 Samuel chapter 4. 1 Samuel 4 tells us that the Philistines slaughtered 30,000 Israelites in a fierce battle. The Philistines also took possession of the Ark of the Covenant during the battle.

It was in this battle that Goliath took part. He was responsible for killing the two wicked sons of the Levite high priest Eli named Hophni and Phinehas, and personally took the Ark of the Covenant to the Philistine city of Ashdod. We know that the prophet who wrote the book in which this battle took place, the prophet Samuel, was a young boy when this battle happened. In 1 Samuel 8:1 we read, "*And it came to pass, when Samuel was old, that he made his sons judges over Israel* (KJV)." At the time of the first mention of Goliath when he challenged Israel to single combat in the Bible, Samuel went from a young man under Eli's tutelage to an old man who was judge and prophet of all Israel. Goliath could have been well past 60 years old by the time he met his death at the hands of King David. His brothers could also have been of an advanced age by the time they met their deaths.

The age of Goliath is important when comparing his current state of health at the time he encountered David. With -GDF-8 and -GDF-11 factors are taken into account we can surmise that Goliath would not be affected by advanced age effects such as muscle deterioration, fatigue, strength deficiency and other aging problems that often occur past the ages of 50 and 60. In all probability Goliath, his brothers, and Og would all have the physical and physiological characteristics of someone in their late 20's to early 30's. We can factor in one other human species characteristics with comparison of aging to that of the descendants of Tsz-Nephilimus Sapien. Neanderthals, as described, have more strength and other physical attributes different than that of modern humans. One other area that is different is in their aging. It is possible that Neanderthals have lived for hundreds of years instead of the mere hundred and some odd years that Homo Sapiens do. We can see this in the unique sloped forehead of some Neanderthal skulls. A sloped forehead develops over a period of hundreds of years. The longer lifespan of Neanderthals is most certainly due to a carry over genetic factor from their older ancestors. Each descendant of an ancestor shares a 31.25% blood relation with a 3rd great grandparent (not referring to a third parent but a great grandfather or grandmother of three generations past). This means that each person born of any human species would have some DNA relations to a great grandparent. This would explain why some children look like, or have traits of family members that their parents don't.

This example of great grandparent ancestry shows that there is a 31.25% chance that genetic drift can bring over genetic traits from someone who lived a lot longer than modern humans. Goliath and Og are just two examples of giants that could have lived far beyond their expected lifetimes. While it is obvious that they eventually would succumb to death, the simple fact remains that Tsz-Nephilimus Sapien and their descendants had many physical and physiological characteristics that made them very unique from the rest of humanity. These genetic varieties are no doubt inherited from the original parentage of Tsz-Nephilimus Sapien.

CHAPTER 11: THE SONS OF GOD & PARENTS OF THE HYBRIDS

It is apparent that Tsz-Nephilimus Sapien and their descendants are very interesting specimens. They are strong, long living, and come with an array of abnormal characteristics. The next thing to consider is from where do they come? A better way of asking this question is who are the parents of Tsz-Nephilimus Sapien? For the answer, then we must look at the term sons of God that Genesis chapter six mentions.

Many people over the centuries have asked the question of who the sons of God are that Genesis six mentions. Many more conservative people have said that the sons of God are the sons of the first man, Adam. However, the answer to who the sons of God are is simple. The sons of God are angels. It has been argued that sons of God actually refers to mankind, or the sons of the nation of Israel as mentioned in Deuteronomy 32:8. This claim is in fact false. Deuteronomy 32:8 uses the term sons of Adam to refer to humans, *"When the most High divided to the nations their inheritance, when He separated the sons of Adam, He set the bounds of the people according to the number of the children of Israel* (KJV)." I researched Deuteronomy 32:8 in several King James Bibles of modern and older times. As a historian and seeker of rare antiquities as I like to consider myself like Indiana Jones, I have collected several rare copies of the Bible that are well past a hundred years old. These Bibles all use the same term *sons of Adam* to refer to mankind just as the modern translations use. The term sons of God is exclusively used to refer to angels.

Angels are defined as a spiritual being found in various religions and mythologies that are often depicted as benevolent celestial beings who act as intermediaries between God and man, or heaven and earth. The word angel comes from a blend of the Old English word *engel,* and Old French *angele.* Both have the same meaning as the late Latin word for angel, *angelus,* which translates into messenger. The Hebrew word for angel is m*al'akh*, which also means messenger. The Hebrew view of angels is messengers with an unspecified nature. The Torah refers to angels as the *Mal'ak Elohim* for angel of God, and the *Bene Elohim* for sons of God. These titles are mentioned in the Jewish Torah and Tanakh.

There are many different kinds of angels. The five main classes are Archangel, Seraphim, Cherubim, Ophanim, Living Creatures, and Ministering Spirits. Ministering Spirits are the ones that primarily interact with mankind in the natural world. Other possible angels are called Dominions, Virtues, Powers, and Principalities. These make up what is called the nine orders of angels. It is likely there are many more types of angels, but these are the known and allegedly known kinds of angels in existence.

*Artistic rendering of an angel.

Angels take many shapes and forms. On earth they often can appear as either divine beings, or in the form of humans. Ministering spirits are the ones that interact with mankind as messengers, teachers, and revealers of things from God. Ministering spirits don't just act as messengers, and other angels could perform other duties if a situation calls for it. Depending on their roles, angels could act as guardians, warring angels, destroyers, and even angels of death. However, this is only speculation, as the actual role of each class is not fully understood.

The best example to use in the understanding that angels have multiple roles is found in 1 Kings 22:19-23. 1 Kings 22:19-23 reads, "*And he said, Hear thou therefore the word of the Lord: I saw the Lord sitting on His throne, and all the host of heaven standing by Him on His right hand and on His left. And the Lord said, who shall persuade Ahab, that he may go up and fall at Ramoth-Gilead? And one said on this manner, and another said on that manner. And there came forth a spirit, and stood before the Lord, and said, I will persuade him. And the Lord said unto him, Where with? And he said, I will go forth, and I will be a lying spirit, in the mouth of all his prophets. And He said, Thou shalt persuade him, and prevail also: go forth, and do so. Now therefore, behold, the Lord hath put a lying spirit in the mouth of all these thy prophets, and the Lord hath spoken evil concerning thee* (KJV)."

This scripture was referring to an incident between the prophet Elijah and King Ahab. We can see that when necessary, the angels of God can volunteer for assignments that are often not a part of their nature. The spirit in the scripture told God that he would become a lying spirit. God does not favor lying, yet allowed the spirit to use lying as a weapon against Ahab.

The different kinds of angels really depends on what authority they hold. Angels of death and destruction would best be considered for powers, dominions, and principalities. Powers is defined as the ability to do something or act in a particular way, especially as a faculty or quality. Dominion is defined as sovereignty and control. Principality is defined as a state ruled by a prince. All of these bodies of authority show that any of the angels in these three categories are ruling types. Every time God used death, destruction, war, and other calamities in the Bible, it was usually done with an angel. Sometimes there would be multiple angels, but often it was just one angel that was needed to do the job of death, destruction, war, and other calamities. Needless to say, angels are very powerful beings.

We now come to the big question of humans and angels. Did angels and humans have sexual relations and produce offspring? The answer to the question is yes. The first thing to understand is the angels who had sex with women were fallen angels, or fallen sons of God. The Bible talks about angels that took wives for themselves and had children with their spouses. Throughout many world cultures are stories of beautiful beings that took human wives for themselves and had offspring with them. The appearance or manifestation of divine beings in Greek and Near Eastern cultures is known as Theophany. Theophany is defined as the appearance of a divine being. It is used to describe God's and godlike beings appearances in religion, mythology, and other accounts of mankind's interactions with supernatural beings.

Major world religions have their share of gods taking human wives and producing offspring. Near and Far Eastern cultures have many beliefs of gods that could resemble the angels of the Bible. In India and China, certain beliefs and worship are centered around snake deities. It is important to point out that while mythology and religion may not be true, the possibility of some truth existing in them is an option to consider. Some stories can often be exaggerated to make what is being told more exciting. Parables in the Bible were taught in a manner that allowed the listener to understand deeper truths that were hidden in a story. It is important to look past the surface of something in order to see the bigger picture.

When considering that angels manifested in the natural world to take spouses for themselves, produce children, and have those children breed and continue their bloodlines, then it is not hard to imagine a connection between the myths, legends, and religious beliefs of gods walking and fornicating among mortal men and women. My belief on fallen angels is that when Lucifer (Satan or the Devil) fell with his angels, and the Bene Elohim that fell after him; that they were mixed with multiple kinds of angels. If we were to look at the Seraphim, then we would see a few interesting observations that are fascinating coincidences with Chinese and Indian snake deities.

Seraphim are worship and guardian angels of the throne of God. According to Isaiah 6:1-3, they have six wings and many eyes covering their entire bodies even underneath their wings. They are described in Isaiah 6:6-7 as using coals and smoke for their work for God. This and other descriptions of the Seraphim have left an impression of them as being fiery in appearance, or using fire materials for their purposes.

The root word of Seraphim, Seraph, has several different meanings. It means noble and high birth like a prince. It means angels who minister. It means priest, or prince of the sanctuary. Seraph also means serpent. The Serpents that are described with the word Seraph often are identified as serpents with wings. We see the use of fiery serpents in Numbers 21:6, "*And the Lord sent fiery serpents among the people, and they bit the people; and much of the people of Israel died* (KJV)."

In Numbers 21:8 it reads, "*And The Lord said unto Moses, Make thee a fiery serpent, and set it on a pole: and it shall come to pass, that every one that is bitten, when he looketh upon it, shall live* (KJV)." This encounter with fiery serpents was because of Israel sinning against God.

Seraphim purify those in the presence of God. Many people consider the serpents that attacked the Israelites as poisonous snakes. However, with the word *fiery* attached to the serpents, this makes it possible that God sent Seraphim among His chosen people to purify them in order to continue being God's chosen people. The emblem that Moses was instructed by God to make to save the people was a fiery serpent. Seeing that the Ark of the Covenant had two Cherubim on top of its mercy seat (or lid) would make it likely that God had Moses construct an image of a Seraphim to purify the people. It should be noted that the image of the fiery serpent God had Moses make was not to be used for worship of the serpent, but to purify the people from their ailment and torment.

In Chinese and Indian mythology and religion is the belief in a group of serpent like people who were divine beings. The word for these creatures is Naga (females is Nagi) in Hinduism, Buddhism, and Jainism. Buddhist and other Chinese religions and myths describe serpents as having other body parts, having human like traits, and possessing extraordinary abilities. Many of the Chinese snake legends speak of them being able to look like serpents one minute, then appearing as humans the next. Often in China these serpents are more commonly thought to be dragons. China contains descriptions of dragons with or without limbs.

The Buddhist Nagas are associated with the Four Heavenly Kings who guard the four cardinal directions of the world. Cardinal directions are the four points on a compass referring to north, south, east, and west. The Four Kings are called in simplified Chinese the Feng Tiao Yu Shun, which means Good Climate. This mention of four kings who watch the cardinal points on the earth is similar to the four angels in Revelation 7:1, "*And after these things I saw four angels standing on the four corners of the earth, holding the four winds of the earth, that the wind should not blow on the earth, nor on the sea, nor on any tree* (KJV)."

These serpent creatures took human wives for themselves and had children with them. While these details don't necessarily mean that the Naga and the Seraphim are one and the same, the Bible does talk about angels being worshiped as gods. 1 Corinthians 10:19-20 states, "*What say I then? That the idol is anything, or that which is offered in sacrifice to idols is anything? But I say, that the things which the Gentiles sacrifice, they sacrifice to devils, and not to God: and I would not that ye should have fellowship with devils* (KJV)." The Bene Elohim who gave birth to the giants are most likely a combination of several of the classes of angels.

The Bible lists angels facing terrible consequences for corrupting their purpose. 2 Peter 2:4 says, *"For if God spared not the angels that sinned, but cast them down to hell, and delivered them into chains of darkness, to be reserved unto judgment* (KJV)."

Jude 1:6 states, *"And the angels which kept not their first estate, but left their own habitation, He hath reserved in everlasting chains under darkness unto the judgment of the great day* (KJV)." The angels who had sexual relations with mankind are mentioned as being found in hell after Jesus visited them.

1 Peter 3:19-20 states, *"By which also He went and preached unto the spirits in prison: Which sometime were disobedient, when once the long suffering of God waited in the days of Noah, while the ark was preparing, wherein few, that is, eight souls were saved by water* (KJV)." Interesting to point out with the 1 Peter scripture is that the Greek words Tartaro and Tartarus are used in place of the word prison. Tartarus is the Greek mythological prison that housed the Titans. The Titans were the parents of the Olympians, and were considered more powerful than the Olympians. The spirits in hell that Jesus visited are believed to be the worst of the worst due to their relationships with the daughters of men.

Angels are created with abilities, powers, and authorities to carry out specific tasks that God has ordained for each kind of angel. They are made to know who God is unlike humans who have to learn about God. They are immortal beings that are privileged to stand in the presence of God while mankind has to learn, believe, and accept Christ in order to attain such relationship with Him.

Angels have free will to choose what they wish to do with their lives. When they choose to do things that are evil, twist their nature, or serve their own interests in a selfish way, then they become fallen. Angels can't be forgiven like mankind for their sins because they already have the knowledge of sin, death, hell, and because they are given many gifts and abilities that mankind can only dream of attaining.

It is not exactly understood why angels and humans can't have unions through marriage and intercourse. Aside from the scriptures and scientific understandings of hybrids mentioned earlier, the best answer to why not is because it would lead to the creation of beings that would be worshipped, idolized, and revered. It would take away the worship of God, remove people seeking His love, and would plunge the world into chaos. The flood of Noah was the very result of such wickedness.

It needs to be understood that while it wasn't the main intention, the hybrids of the Bene Elohim and humanity created people of incredible size, strength, age, and other superior traits. These people would become as Genesis six describes as the heroes of old, and the men of renown. Why would humans marry angels and have sexual relations with them? The answer is because they are beautiful beings.

Angels can look like humans, but can also look like creatures of extraordinary looks and abilities. Angels can also bring comfort, insight, revelation, and judgment to people. King David saw an angel hovering over Jerusalem before it brought a plague to the people. The Prophet Elisha witnessed an army of flaming chariots and horses prepped for war. The mother of Ishmael, Hagar, saw an angel in the wilderness who gave her comfort and prophecy over her son when she was running away from Abraham and Sarah while she was pregnant with Ishmael. Angels comforted Jesus after His trials in the wilderness with Satan, and again during His preparation for crucifixion after the Passover feast.

Imagine coming into contact with one of these types of

angels. Instead of doing God's work, they use their knowledge and beauty to make you feel a sense of wonder and awe. They speak words that are comforting to you, and make you feel safe with them. Imagine the possibility of falling in love with that angel. The Bene Elohim were attracted to the beauty of the daughters of men, but it was possibly what the women saw and heard from the angels that made them become their wives. 2 Corinthians 11:14-15 says, *"And no marvel; for Satan himself is transformed into an angel of light. Therefore it is no great thing if his ministers also be transformed as the ministers of righteousness; whose end shall be according to their works* (KJV)." Fallen angels can disguise themselves as angels of light. It is likely the Bene Elohim were not fallen when they first went to the earth. But, they did become fallen once they took their wives from mankind. Why would angels commit the acts of sin that would lead them to be bound up in chains of doom and gloom when they knew what would happen to them. The answer is because they could.

The ability to do something is a powerful impulse. If the impulse is strong enough, then it could turn into addiction. Angels are as susceptible to this mentality as humans. An example of this is found in the desire of angels to have the revelations and relationships with the Holy Spirit like mankind does. 1 Peter 1:12 states, *"Unto whom it was revealed, that not unto themselves, but unto us they did minister the things, which are now reported unto you by them that have preached the gospel unto you with the Holy Ghost sent down from heaven; which things the angels desire to look into* (KJV)." Desire, passion, comfort, thrill, lust, love or the illusion of love can make anyone seek to possess and commit acts that could be a mistake. This was the reason the sons of God married into mankind, had children, and fell. Sometimes, the act of doing nothing is enough to stay out of trouble.

CHAPTER 12: EXTINCTION OR ADAPTION?

Did Tsz-Nephilimus Sapien become extinct like so many other human species? Did they adapt to the changing times to keep up with Homo Sapiens? What became of a species that at one time thrived on earth is not entirely understood. What is known is the human body can adapt to almost anything even far down at the cellular level.

Extinction is defined in biological and ecological instances of the end of an organism or group of organisms (called a taxon). Adaption (or adaptive trait) is a biological term for a trait with a current functional role in the life of an organism that is maintained and evolved by means of natural selection. Adaption can enhance fitness and survival abilities of individuals. When entering into a new environment, a single genotype can produce new phenotypes that will help the body adapt to its new environment. When taking into account hybrid genetics, then the possibilities of their phenotypes and environments is an unknown minefield. Hybrids have difficulty in reproduction. Two different species produce offspring that often don't have enough genetic material for proper procreation. Many hybrids such as feline hybrids of Ligers (father is a male lion and mother is a female tiger or tigress) and Tigons (father is a male tiger and mother is a female lion or lioness) often produce offspring that are infertile. However, many species of hybrids have been very fertile and produced viable offspring.

The famous Killer Bee is a hybrid Bee species that is the result of crossbreeding African Honey Bees with European Honey Bees. After escaping containment in Brazil in 1957, the Killer Bees, or Africanized Honey Bees as they are classified, spread across South, Central, and North America and have produced multiple species that all stemmed from a single collection of hybrid honey bees. An interesting point of topic on Ligers, Tigons, and Killer Bees is that they are all larger than their host parents. This is due to the growth inhibitor genes in the big cats being suppressed, and a possible connection to an ancestor in the bees lineage that stems from Africa. Life finds ways of making all things go from the impossible to the possible.

2 Peter 2:6 states, *"And turning the cities of Sodom and Gomorrha into ashes condemned them with an overthrow, making them an example unto those that after should live ungodly… (KJV)."* The word extinction is used in place of overthrow in some Bible translations. Sodom and Gomorrha were wicked cities that God wiped off the face of the planet. The most logical idea of what happened to the whole area of the cities and its inhabitants is they succumbed to hydrothermal circulation. Hydrothermal circulation is when hot water circulates around areas of extreme heat most often the result of volcanic

activity. Hydrothermal circulation causes ore genesis that creates the various minerals found within the earth's crust and other areas that contain valuable minerals and ores. The process creates many valuable metals and ores, but can also create phosphate. Phosphate is an inorganic chemical and a *salt* of phosphoric acid. Phosphate is a solid material that is mined all over the world. Several phosphate mines can be found in the American states of Utah and Florida, and in the African countries of Morocco and Tunisia. Phosphate can also be found in Egypt, Israel, Jordan, Syria, Iraq, Iran, and Saudi Arabia. Sodom and Gomorrha were believed to be in areas where the Dead Sea is today.

In Genesis 19, the wife of a man named Lot was turned into a pillar of salt after looking back at the destruction of Sodom and Gomorrha. Lot's wife succumbed to fractional crystallization. The removal of water, carbon dioxide, hydrogen, and oxygen add to the composition change in fractional crystallization. The people, flora, fauna, and buildings of Sodom and Gomorrha most certainly succumbed to the same fate as Lot's wife. This would cause brecciation, rock composed of broken minerals and rock fragments cemented together by fine-grained groundmasses (also called matrixes) of fragment composition, to occur and make all the rock formations and mines found through the areas of the Dead Sea and surrounding areas.

The mention of Sodom and Gomorrha is to show that the Bible has extinction level events that have to do with the destruction of entire people so that none ever rise again. Lot's own daughters lost their chance at husbands in the destruction of Sodom and Gomorrha. They were so desperate for the continuation of their bloodline that they got Lot drunk and had sexual relations with their own father just to satisfy their desire for children. While disgusting and perverse, the point to be made is that there was not one male in the entire region left for Lot's daughters to reproduce with and have offspring (or at least that is what the daughters feared had happened). Lot was from the land of Ur (the same as Abraham whose family Lot came from) and a foreigner in Sodom and Gomorrha. That is why he was allowed to live. Everything else that was apart of the land that these two cities occupied was obliterated and made extinct.

We don't see giants walking around in masses today. Most likely the original Tsz-Nephilimus Sapiens and their descendants all but died out. However, death does not mean extinct. Death is an end for some, but descendants can carry on the genetics of someone who has died into a new generation. If Og was the last of the original hybrids, then that made his species completely extinct. However, Og probably had some children of his own. They would be watered down genetically, but would carry some of the DNA of Og's original people. Goliath and his brothers carried genetics of the original giants. The Scythians, Chinese giants, and so on all had the genetics of their original host parents flowing in their veins. It has been discovered recently that many extinct human species such as Neanderthals had children with Homo Sapiens. While Neanderthals are extinct, some of their genetics no doubt still exist within some of their Homo-Sapien descendants. This too can be likely with the giants.

I remember one time when I was at my gym having a conversation with a US Army veteran. He was an army medic that served in Afghanistan for a couple of tours. The veteran was a massive man. He was an accomplished bodybuilder that could rival many of the professionals that I watch on stage at competitions. He was familiar with the Genesis six hybrids from his readings of the Bible. He told me about a unit of Afghanistan soldiers that his unit was attached to for assignments in some of the local areas. He described these men as huge men unlike the usual sized

Afghan soldiers he noticed. He described them as large, strong, and lovers of war. He said if he did not know any better that those men could have been Nephilim descendants just by how ferocious they were in combat. I have seen pictures of many giants in Afghanistan. Some most likely had gigantism and acromegaly, but others looked like they were able to move as easy as an average sized man.

Life can change almost over night. All organisms can go from one stage of life to another if they can adapt to whatever situation they encounter. The Ice Age is believed to have ended 12,000 years ago. I have mentioned the possibility of the Bible spanning a timeline of almost 10,000 years. If we look at the possibilities of large layers of ice melting slowly over thousands of years, then have a major event such as the flood of Noah with not only rain, but volcanic eruptions, and earthquakes (Genesis 7:11) speeding up the melting of the large masses of ice that would possibly be left melting from the last few remnants of the Ice Age; it would explain a great deal of how so much water could accumulate to cover the earth and help move the masses of the Pangean super continent to where today's continents are located. There is a belief that Earth had a canopy of water or moisture surrounding it before the flood, which at some point became the rain that lasted for forty days and nights during the flood. I believe the rain did come from a moisture canopy, but was only the first step in creating the massive floodwaters that covered the entirety of the earth.

It's likely the Pangea was already moving at a rate of separation, but the impact of the flood waters and the volcanic activity resulting from tectonic plates shifting would add greatly to the movement of the continents similar to the earthquake that moved the island of Japan eight feet from where it was in the year 2011 (and also changing the earths axis in the process). The last remnants of other human species also began to go extinct around the end of the Ice

Age. This is very likely the result of the part of Genesis six before the flood when God said man would eventually live to be no more than 120 years of age (meaning environmental factors had already begun to take effect on mankind).

The only way that any other human species would survive extinction would be through genetic drift by way of a small percentage of their genetic material to survive into the other people who survived the flood. If Og survived the flood, then he most likely could have had children with his species genetics still in their blood. If there were other hybrids made (as Genesis six makes clear that the Bene Elohim did go forth after the flood to have some more offspring), then there would still be new amounts of Tsz-Nephilimus Sapiens DNA to once again use to make more giants. However, the environmental and ecological changes to the earth done by the effects of the flood would add to the slow extinction of the whole of the bloodlines of Tsz-Nephilimus Sapien. If any adaption took place into modern times, then it would be found in the genetics of some of the people living today. The question to ask is how much, if any, is left of Tsz-Nephilimus Sapien, and will we ever see them again?

CHAPTER 13: FIELD NOTES

There are always questions that are left to be answered in any venture undertaken. When people learn about something, then they naturally have questions that they wish to be answered to gain a better understanding of what they just learned. In this final chapter I will put together some of the other discoveries and theories that I have uncovered in my research. It is important to show some of the things that will help further a person's viewpoint, and to help expand their thoughts on a particular subject to help them in their own time of study and meditation.

Are there any remains or fossils of Tsz-Nephilimus Sapien that have been discovered? The answer is a mixed answer of yes and no. The alleged findings of giant skeletons and remains have basically been nothing but bogus claims by people either with little to no real proof. Most pictures on the internet are nothing more than photo-shopped pictures. Any real evidence has been alleged to be apart of the usual cover up and conspiracy/theory ideas. The best evidence that has been actually publicized has been found in Russia, China, and Indonesia. These findings however are only small fragments of unique skeletal remains either buried in graves or mounds called Kurgans, found in caves, or found in sites that are not often graves (some findings of people are those who most likely died and were not buried except by natural elements over time). China has some of the most amazing ancient civilizations that are still being discovered. Many of the recent archeological findings have yet to be identified with any of the already known people and dynasties found in China's history.

The province of Xinjiang, China has burial sites such as the Kungang tomb (ancient name of the Aral region of Xinjiang) where a long coffin was found containing a male giant that may have been even taller when he was alive (the body shrinks after death because skin dries out due to lack of fluids and water). While only one body was discovered, the point is that some possible remains of giants have been found. Near Surakarta in Central Java, Indonesia in the Sangiran archaeological site are discoveries of skull and mandible (lower jaw) parts of an alleged human species named Meganthropus (Meganthropus Palaeojavanicus is a genus name similar to Tsz-Nephilimus Sapien by way of the species still being largely unknown in the science community and not completely accepted as its official title yet). Meganthropus species is between 9 and 10 feet tall. This human species is still being studied as only a few small remains have been discovered. The thing to understand about remains is that bodies that are not buried with proper techniques decompose over time. Bones are as easily susceptible to decomposing. After a little longer period of time, bones not properly preserved can gradually decompose (faster if they are being consumed by fungi and bacteria that has formed from attraction by decomposing flesh). Finding actual remains of any human or animal skeletons is difficult. This is also true for giants. Have people found ancient giant remains that could be Tsz-Nephilimus Sapien or their descendants? Yes. Is it known completely if they are giants of this extinct species? No.

Were all of the giants evil? The answer would be no. Looking at the terminology used in Genesis 6:4 to describe the giants as mighty men who were of old, and men of renown gives us some insight into at least some of their character traits. Some translations use the term heroes in place of men. Using the Greek hero Heracles, The Urian king Gilgamesh, and a few of the later believed descendants from the Roman Empire such as Maximinus Thrax (a foreign Roman Emperor with a mother of alleged Iranian-Scythian/Sarmatian descent who ruled Rome for three years without ever actually setting foot in Rome), then we have a few individuals who were at the least men who tried to do good things. None of these men were what I'd call great or righteous human beings.

Heracles killed people he shouldn't have such as his music teacher. Gilgamesh neglected many of his duties by seeking immortality. Maximinus was a warlord by all accounts, but according to their biographies they at least tried to do what could be considered good during their lifetimes. Heracles lived his life to fix a lot of problems in the world. Gilgamesh sought to save the life of his friends by helping them live forever. Maximinus being born a common man and soldier before becoming emperor, raised the pay of soldiers and sought to remove the politically corrupt nobility from power in Rome (he hated the Roman nobility and was ruthless against them in terms of eliminating or limiting their power). These men are not perfect, but the point of their mention is that some of the giants were at least not raving monsters, but men who tried to be good leaders (albeit with a lot of failures to their credit as rulers). I find the research on Maximinus Thrax interesting as he was said to be over eight feet tall (8 feet and six inches is his exact estimated height), was strong enough to pull a laden cart by himself, and could kill a horse with a single punch (to the head). His heritage linking back to the Scythians is also of interest as it adds more depth of my views on the Scythians.

Are there female angels or daughters of God? There are two scriptures in the Bible that advocate the possibility of female angels, or in Hebrew the *Hbnvt Shl Lvhym* (Elohim). Zechariah 5:9 states, *"Then I lifted up mine eyes, and looked, and, behold, there came out two women, and the wind was in their wings; for they had wings like the wings of a stork: and they lifted up the ephah (basket) between the earth and the heavens (KJV)."* This scripture refers to angels that resemble women who have not fallen like the sons of God. Then, Isaiah 34:14 says, *"The wild beasts of the desert shall also meet with the wild beasts of the island, and the satyr shall cry to his fellow; the screech owl also shall rest there, and find for herself a place of rest (KJV)."*

The screech owl is referred to in the Hebrew Bible and other Bible translations as Lilith or night demon. This often represents a female spirit that is often described as evil and rapacious (greedy or grasping). These two scriptures are the only two in the Bible that mention angels and demons with female characteristics and a female name. Whether they had relationships with the sons of Adam is not known. But, there have been accounts where people have witnessed what appear to be female angels outside of the two mentioned Bible verses. Because of these two verses and eyewitness accounts, it is safe to say that there are female angels in existence, or at least angels that take on a female form when on the earth. Angels don't have a defined gender like mankind does, but because they are identified by gender terminology shows they can be male and female. There were also female giants as the offspring were both male and female genders.

Did Tsz-Nephilimus Sapien and their descendants die and become demons and evil spirits? This is a new belief that is floating around in the world. One word that describes a later generation of giants is Rephaite or Rephaim (Rephaim is used by both Hebrew and Phoenician languages). The Hebrew definition (of both words) means giant, and the dead ones (dead ancestors is also a confirmed definition). The dead ones refers to residents of the Netherworld (hell or sheol which is Hebrew for the grave). The Bible makes use of the term dead ones and ancestors in the books of Isaiah, Psalms, Proverbs, Job, and 2 Chronicles. It is believed that upon death, the giants became evil spirits and thus the name Rephaim has been associated with them for both a term of giant while living, and evil spirit when they died. The evidence and research for this claim is very meager. Due to this and the need for further research, the possibility of the giants becoming evil spirits is unknown.

In the movie *Captain America The Winter Soldier*, a villain named Baron Von Strucker comments on the age that the world has entered. He says, "It's not an age of spies anymore, not even an age of heroes. It is the age of miracles. There is nothing more horrifying than a miracle!" The possibility of a species being born of an angel and human union would be considered a miracle to many people. Many people would consider that a horrifying predicament.

Many people don't believe in the idea of giants, hybrids, or angels and humans having sexual relations. However, the Bible and history provide many accounts that can make it reality. It is not easy to believe in the things that many people have yet to see a lot of proof exists or existed. However, Jesus once said blessed are those that haven't seen Him (after His resurrection from the grave) and still chose to believe He rose from the grave (John 20:29). When one takes the leap of faith into the unknown, then they have taken one step further to becoming more like God, whom mankind was made in the image of in the first place. That is one of the greater testaments of faith anyone can ever attain. As Hebrews 11:1 states, "*Now faith is the substance of things hoped for, the evidence of things not seen* (KJV)." Faith leads us to know the things of the unknown.

ABOUT THE AUTHOR

Dr. Harry Assad Salem III is an author of several books dealing with theology, archaeology, religion, history, and science. He holds state, regional, national, and world championships in the sports of powerlifting and strongman. He is also an NPC bodybuilder.

Dr. Salem holds five doctorate degrees in the fields of theology, archaeology, Biblical studies, Christian education, and practical ministry. He has been involved in ministry since the age of thirteen with Salem Family Ministries. He has lectured at School of Worship for several years. He has developed a children's book series called Prayer Buddies with two books published called Count of Ten Say Amen and Ten Steps to Build and be Spirit Filled.

Dr. Salem is an advocate of education who believes that the highest goals one can achieve can be reached through knowledge and skills learned in the classroom or on the job, and applied in the world to gain experience and mastery over anything and everything. Dr. Salem's personal motto and creed is, "Excellence is excellent." It is a belief that has kept him thriving for the highest of excellence in every pursuit he has worked towards. He hopes to inspire others to achieve their own pursuits of excellence, foster climates of change in their lives, and live to their fullest potential in everyway possible. He has one niece, Mia Gabrielle Salem, and one nephew, Roman Harry Salem Jr.

Sources for Photos:

Cover Photo, Merodach-Baladan King of Babylon, Courtesy of Scewing PD-US

Pg. 16, New Species Creation Chart made by Dr. Harry Salem III

Pg. 32, Pangea Photo Courtesy of en.user:Kieff CC-BY-SA 3.0

Pg. 36, Map Courtesy of John D. Croft CC-BY-SA 3.0

Pg. 47, Gilgamesh Courtesy of the Louvre Museum in Paris, France PD-US

Pg. 52, Heracles statue, courtesy of photographer Yair Haklai CC-BY-SA 2.5

Pg. 61, Greek gold comb depiction of Scythians in battle Courtesy of Maqs PD-US

Pg. 69, Photo by John Thompson from Illustrations of China and its People 1873-74 PD-US

Pg. 99, Warrior Vase Courtesy of Sharon Mollerus CC-BY-2.0

Pg. 118, Postaxial Polydactyly right hand x-ray courtesy of Magnus Manske CC-BY-3.0

Pg. 125, Unknown Tomb photo courtesy of photographer Josef Wagner, Penn Museum PERMISSION BY OWNER

Pg. 131, Artist Rendering of an angel by Dr. Harry Salem III

*All photos listed above and through chapters are either owned by the author, public domain, or have been given permission by the owner or photographer for use in this book provided all credit is given to appropriate parties. Most photos are made available by Wikipedia and Wikimedia.

I would love to hear from you. There are many ways to stay connected to me. You can contact me either through the mail or the internet at the ministry website.

Salem Family Ministries

P.O. Box 1595

Cathedral City, CA 92234

www.salemfamilyministries.org

Dr. Harry Assad Salem III

www.ingramcontent.com/pod-product-compliance
Lightning Source LLC
Chambersburg PA
CBHW071220090426
42736CB00014B/2915